WE HAVE THIS HOPE

JONATHAN GALLAGHER

Pacific Press Publishing Association
Boise, Idaho
Oshawa, Ontario, Canada

Edited by David Jarnes/Jerry D. Thomas
Designed by Tim Larson
Cover photos by John Baker and Betty Blue
Typeset in 10/12 Century Schoolbook

Unless otherwise noted, all Scripture references are from the New International Version.

The author assumes responsibility for the accuracy of all quotations cited in this book.

Library of Congress Cataloging-in-Publication Data:
Gallagher, Jonathan, 1952-
　　　We have this hope / Jonathan Gallagher.
　　　　　p.　　cm.
　　　ISBN 0-8163-1142-0
　　　1. Bible. N.T. Timothy, 1st—Criticism, interpretation,
etc. 2. Bible. N.T. Titus—Criticism, interpretation, etc.
3. Hope—Religious aspects—Christianity. 4. Christian
life—1960-
I. Title.
BS2745.2.G35　　1993
227'.8306—dc20　　　　　　　　　　　　　　　92—42961
　　　　　　　　　　　　　　　　　　　　　　　　　　CIP

93 94 95 96 97 ● 5 4 3 2 1

Contents

7/93

Hope: The First Word

"Who wants to live forever?" sang British rock group Queen in 1986, voicing the widespread view that life is meaningless. And if living forever means eternal life in this despairing, perverted world, then who would disagree? Who would want a never-ending experience of evil, hatred, and self-destruction? Such an "eternal life" would be more like the eternal hell of Greek mythology, with the accursed doomed to meaningless suffering, endlessly repeated—like Prometheus, the fire-stealing Titan, sentenced to be chained to a rock where every day an eagle tore out and devoured his liver, and every night it was miraculously restored.

Who wants to live forever if that is life and there's no way out except death, nothing better than nonexistence, no answers to life's big questions? If that's all there is to life, the nothingness exit of suicide seems the best choice.

But if to live forever means an eternity in God's presence, the promise of a recreated humanity, the happiness of a transformed society, the assurance of an earth made new, a place where only righteousness dwells and every being freely chooses good—what then?

Ah then, who *wouldn't* want to live forever? And that *is* the offer God makes to all who come to Him for healing salvation! That's what gives meaning to our existence. That's the hope of us who are born dying—the hope of eternal life.

God's hope for our hopelessness, hope that is sure and certain, hope that is based on the cast-iron guarantee of God Himself—

this is *the* hope!

I once conducted the graveside service for a church member while another interment proceeded nearby. The member had lived a long and fulfilled life and had fallen asleep in his loving Lord Jesus. While there were tears and a sense of loss because of the separation, the mourners showed their trusting hope in the Lord of the resurrection.

What a contrast the other service made! With shriekings and wailings, this group grieved as those who have no hope. As far as they were concerned, this was it: The one they loved was forever gone.

It is on occasions such as these that the Christian message really makes a difference. In hospitals and at bedsides I have had many talks with those who were expecting death. In the fragility of our lives, only God's hope can make a difference.

The meaning of hope

So what is hope? We say, "I hope you'll understand me." "I hope it doesn't rain tomorrow." "I hope I'll find a good job." Here hope has the sense of faint expectation—"I would like it to happen; it probably won't, but I still 'hope.'"

It's probably this negative view of hope that has given birth to some of our proverbs: "Who lives by hope will die by hunger"; "Too much hope deceives."

Many of the world's great writers didn't regard hope any more favorably. The Latin writer Gratian proclaimed, "Hope is a great falsifier of the truth," and the German philosopher Nietzsche was even more pessimistic: "Hope in reality is the worst of all evils, because it prolongs the torment of man."

So what then of the Christian hope? On what is it based?

If I promise to come and visit you, would you expect me? Depends on my record, doesn't it? God has promised eternal life. Can we expect that promise to be fulfilled? Well, what kind of person is God? Does He make false promises? Can He lie? No! Our hope is an absolutely sure and certain hope because of the Person who stands behind it.

This hope is the fundamental motivation of the Christian. It gives us a reason for living; it gives direction to our lives.

Without this hope, we're lost.

Biblical hope

Hope is a recurring theme of 1 Timothy and Titus, the epistles that underlie our study here. In the very first verse of 1 Timothy, Paul identifies the basis of our hope: The "Lord Jesus Christ . . . is our hope." Later in the same letter, he repeats this theme: "We have put our hope in the living God, who is the Savior of all men" (1 Timothy 4:10).

In the second verse of Titus, Paul refers to both the result of our hope and its basis: "The hope of eternal life, which God, who does not lie, promised before the beginning of time." And in the next chapter, he writes of our "blessed hope, . . . the glorious appearing of the great God and our Saviour Jesus Christ" (Titus 2:13, KJV).

Hope is an important theme of other parts of the New Testament as well. Acts 24:15 speaks of our "hope . . . that there will be a resurrection of both the righteous and the wicked." Romans 8:25 emphasizes the patience hope implies as we wait for something we do not yet have. Romans 12:12 speaks of "rejoicing in hope" (KJV), and 2 Corinthians 3:12 points out "since we have such a hope, we are very bold" (NIV).

Galatians 5:5 speaks of "the righteousness for which we hope," Colossians 1:27 says that "Christ in you [is] the hope of glory," Hebrews 6:19 describes it "as an anchor for the soul, firm and secure," and 1 Peter 1:3 says that it is "the resurrection of Jesus Christ" that provides our hope.

How amazing and important hope is! Romans 8:24 even goes so far as to say that "we are saved by hope" (KJV). Do you begin to see the meaning of this hope that is centered on the Almighty God Himself? If you do not have this hope, how can you face the future? How can you live in the present?

Who is this God of hope?

But the hope you have depends on the kind of God you hope in!

One day as I was sitting in a church, listening as the organist practiced, a young lady asked to see me. Approaching me, she sat for some time without speaking. Then, her face turned away, her eyes closed, she said, "I don't hope anymore. There's nothing left. I've tried it all."

"But—"

"But nothing. Listen—I know you're a minister, but there's nothing you can tell me that will make any difference. Especially about God. No hope there. None at all."

The swirling chords of the organ moved between us, preventing a response—not that she was listening to me anyway.

Eventually she went on: "Oh, I know He's there. I know He's watching me. And I know He's going to get me. *That's* why I have no hope. He demands that I do what He says—or else. I can't love Him. And because I can't, He's going to burn me in the lake of fire. Don't talk to me about hope. It's hopeless."

And in tears she fled the church.

How clearly this demonstrates that it is the *character of your God* that determines whether you have hope. If you regard God as harsh and vindictive, then what can you hope for except that extinction will come quickly?

No, real hope must be based on something sure—and attractive! How could I help this young woman? How could I share my hope? I could only do so by sharing my own experience of the God of hope, by introducing her to the person I know Him to be.

Still crying, the young lady came back into the church and sat down again. And listened. I comforted and quietly spoke of my God of hope. And in spite of her despair, hope grew again: hope in the true God of hope who saves us by hope in the blessed hope!

A half-smile dawned through the still-questioning, wet eyes; she started anew with the God who offers His hope.

This book

Why this book? It attempts to reveal why Paul wrote the way he did to Timothy and Titus; it aims to express the foundation of the Christian's objective—the truly blessed hope—and to show the way to live in such a hope. And hopefully, it will lead us all to a deeper conviction of the importance of the God of hope in our individual lives and of our future with Him for all eternity.

CHAPTER 1

7/93

The God of Relationships

1 Timothy 1:1, 2; Titus 1:4

Recently, I took a sampling of passersby on the question "What do you think about God?" The answers varied widely:

"I couldn't say I really believe in a God."

"Just look around you—don't talk to me about God. More like a vicious devil. Me? I'm just waiting for the hammer to fall."

"Ah, yes. The absolute essence, the great expression of unachievability, the transcendent unknowing. Our hope must be to be absorbed into the energy of the One."

"You'd better believe in Him. Otherwise you're doomed. He's the righteous Judge who holds the keys of Hell and Death, who comes to punish all unrighteousness. If you don't want to be burned forever, you'd just better believe!"

"God for me is the inner power of the universe, and we need to tune into these mystic vibrations so that we can be transformed and become God too. Good karma."

"Ah, the Divine Being. The sum of our aspirations, the description of what is good in ourselves, the elevation of the human spirit. If only all the world could live as one in the brotherhood of mankind."

"God? What did He ever do for me?"

"God—of course I believe in God. Just do as He says, and you'll begin your ascent of the astral planes."

Lots of thoughts about God out there, but hardly any consistency! It's as if the eyes of the people of the world have been blinded so that they will believe almost anything at all—which is why so many have concluded that religious beliefs are simply human hopes and wishes.

Yet, as Eugene O'Neill wrote, "When men make gods, there is no God." The truth is that people today understand as little of God as did those of the first-century world into which Jesus came.

Hope and relationships

The Greeks and Romans of Jesus' time conceived of hundreds of gods and goddesses, but their divinities offered little in the way of inspiration. Zeus, for instance—known to the Romans as Jupiter—was the offspring of the Titan Cronus, who had married his sister Rhea. Warned by the Fates that one of his children was destined to overthrow him, Cronus swallowed each child at birth. Zeus, however, was concealed from Cronus, and eventually fought with and castrated his father. Zeus had many female consorts and often took the form of birds or animals to seduce human women.

Near the time of Jesus' birth, the mystery religions arose as a reaction to the nonsensical myths about the gods of the traditional pagan religions. Mithraism (a kind of sun worship) and the cults of Isis and Cybele (eastern fertility goddesses) stressed secret knowledge gained only by the initiated. These religions offered hypnotic, frenzied activities through which one could be filled by the god worshiped.

At this time, the old revelation through the Law and the Prophets was so distorted as to offer little comfort. It was locked up in the rituals and ceremonies for which the Jews were famous: a cold and joyless religion of observance and rules, the "commandments of men."

Like people of every age, the people of the first century were looking for something that would give them meaning and purpose. Many of them had come to regard their religious beliefs as irrelevant and pointless. The old pagan gods not only failed to convince, they could hardly engender admiration or reverence from their human worshipers. Nor could they encourage any kind of moral worth. The newer "mystery religions" brought some momentary excitement to the senses, but were devoid of believable truth. And the religion of rules and traditions offered little comfort for people searching for meaning and personal help.

This was the world into which Christianity entered—like a bombshell. How it differed from such perverse and perverted ideas of God—teaching that God had come to this world, had died at human hands, had risen again, and would grant eternal life to all who loved Him. It was mind shattering!

No wonder then that Paul begins his letter to Timothy with this clear designation of the Christian's primary hope: "God our Savior and . . . Christ Jesus our hope" (1 Timothy 1:1). To him the "blessed hope" was not a dry, formal doctrine, but part of the living relationship between us and God and between us and other people.

Paul addresses both Timothy and Titus as his true sons "in the faith" (see 1 Timothy 1:2; Titus 1:4). Both of them were to the aging apostle assurances that the hope he gave his life for would continue to be preached, that the vital message of God's truly *good* news would continue to inspire and change those who would hear and respond.

Hope is an essential part of the relationship that binds God to people and people to their fellow human beings. Without hope, these relationships would not exist.

The promise of Immanuel

I have a nephew named Emanuel. My wife's family comes from Madeira, where Emanuel (one *m*!) is a common Christian name. So whenever I sing

> We're marching through Immanuel's ground,
> To fairer worlds on high

or

> O come, O come, Immanuel,
> And ransom captive Israel

it's hard for me not to visualize a young face full of mischief and fun, a boy (now grown) who liked to climb trees and play games and get dirty. Yet "wonder child" though he is—every child is a wonder of God—my nephew Emanuel is not the real Immanuel, "God with us."

God's promise to be with us is surely the most amazing fact of Christianity. From the very beginning, when God met with Adam and Eve in the garden, He has been trying to live with us, to *be* with us. In the pillar of smoke by day and the pillar of fire by night, God showed the Israelites He was really with them. In the smoke, thunder, and lightning of Mount Sinai, God demonstrated His presence. And when Moses came down from the mount, his face gleamed with the glory of being with God. So, too, in the shekinah glory that filled Solomon's temple, God said, "I am with you."

Yet, all this was not enough. All the symbols and signs, all the thunder and lightning, could not truly express God's presence. Not even the glorious temple nor the ark of the covenant could adequately communicate His presence with us. So "God sent his Son." Isaiah 7:14 and 8:8 name this one to come "Immanuel"—God with us.

He is here. God is now present with fallen humanity. He has arrived. Jesus' life and death and resurrection offer proof of the truth of His name. Yet strangely enough, apart from that brief reference in Matthew, Jesus is never referred to as Immanuel.

Why not?

Because though He was truly God with us, Jesus came not as the glorious king but as the suffering servant—a man among men, human. As such, He was limited, restricted, subject to the same pains and sicknesses, the same troubles and temptations as all the rest of us. And this Jesus, this God with us, died with us as a criminal nailed to a cross.

Jesus' birth in Bethlehem marked the beginning of "God with us," but we haven't yet seen the full reality. After thirty short years, the bodily presence of Immanuel was ended—first by the crucifixion and then by the ascension. What then of this "God with us," of the One who was promised to live with humanity?

Only in Immanuel's return will the promise be made complete.

The God who helps and cares

Jesus' second advent is the last act in the drama of "For God so loved the world that he *gave* his one and only Son" (John 3:16,

emphasis supplied). Jesus comes the second time in all His
glory as majestic proof of the immensity of God's love for us, the
completing contrast to His former coming to die in love so that
we might live. This is the truth of Jesus' return; this is what it
means.

If Jesus' coming is no less a demonstration of love than His
death on the cross, it is hard to see why some fear His return.
God created us because of His nature of love. His love demands
that the chasm sin dug be bridged so that we may again live in
His presence. This is truly a "blessed hope"; only those who have
no love for God would wish Him not to return. It is only those
who refuse His love and help who call for the mountains and
rocks to hide them from Him.

But while God is love, He is not weak. At times we may be
tempted to view Him as an indulgent uncle who cares for us so
much that we can do as we please. We may even want to assume
the responsibility for the second coming itself by implying that
Jesus can come only when we are ready. In this we make Jesus
Christ subject to our summons, "calling him down out of heaven"
as it suits our purpose. We must be absolutely clear that it is
God who promises the second advent and that we cannot control
His plans by appealing to a mistaken notion of His indulgence.

God is "patient with you, not wanting anyone to perish, but
everyone to come to repentance" (2 Peter 3:9). But genuine love
is not sick sentimentality that does nothing. Love ultimately
demonstrates its authenticity by dramatic intervention: "The
day of the Lord *will* come" (2 Peter 3:10, KJV, emphasis supplied), and those who have failed to respond to the returning
Lord's love and grace will find themselves unready to welcome
Him, condemned by their own lovelessness.

The promise of Christ's second coming offers assurance precisely because it is totally out of the hands of feeble, arrogant
humanity. From the very beginning it has been God who acts for
us. We do not lift ourselves up to God. He reaches down to bring
us to Himself. That is the symbolism of the second coming—
God's activity for fallen humanity. God initiates, we react. He
offers, we accept. He reaches out, we take His hand. "Salvation
is of the Lord," says the second coming; we do not engineer it.

And because the second advent depends on *His* initiative, we don't have to worry. Our responsibility is simply to actively respond to His call and to actively "occupy" until He comes. The second coming is firmly based in the loving, caring nature of God Himself, which leaves no room for doubt. It is the final act in the plan of salvation promised by the God who cares, the God who came and died at our hands so that we might live.

Are we alone now?

So, are we alone now? In placing the stress on the Christ to come, do we forget the assurance "I am with you always, even to the very end of the age"? In emphasizing "I will come again," do we ignore "where two or three come together in my name, there am I with them"? Do our eyes strain so hard to see that "redemption is drawing near" that we miss seeing "that Christ may dwell in your hearts through faith" (Matthew 28:30; John 14:3, KJV; Matthew 18:20; Luke 21:28; Ephesians 3:17)?

Is our Immanuel up there or down here? If we see only an external Christ who comes on the clouds of heaven at the end, then we live alone. Then, until Jesus comes, our everyday lives have no meaning. And we do not know our Lord because we do not see Him in our hearts or in the lives of others.

When Jesus told a picture story of the end, of judgment and separation, the "goats" were excluded not because of what they claimed, but because the Lord did not know them. Why not? Because they had not recognized their Lord in the sick, the suffering, the imprisoned. We must see Jesus now, active in our lives and pleading in the eyes of the needy.

On the other hand, if we see only an internal Christ, then what hope do we have? Where is the promised end to suffering and death? Where is the blessed hope? If Christ does not come again to terminate sin and evil, then there is no point to life at all. His first coming as Immanuel would be turned into a mockery and a sham because His power and presence would remain forever incomplete. Without Jesus' return, 'God with us' is a dream only half realized.

When I speak to my friend Jim on the phone, he is present on the other end of the line. He is real, and I truly believe I'm speaking to a literal person and not someone I've made up. But sometimes this presence is less than satisfactory. At times the line is bad, and I'm not exactly sure what he says. At times I want more than just his words; I want to see his face, to see how he reacts to what I'm saying. Ultimately, a phone conversation is a poor substitute for the real thing—face-to-face talking.

So too with God. He's always wanted to speak directly with the beings He created. But sin separated humanity from His presence. Yet ever since He banished Adam and Eve from the Garden, God has been working toward restoring that lost communion, toward bringing us back to be with Him.

So while it is true that we enter into eternal life now and we commune with our Lord now, we will experience full communion with Him only when we meet Him "face to face." Jesus *is* present with us *now*, but only spiritually, invisibly, indefinably. Jesus will be present with us *then* literally, visibly, unarguably. We can experience His true presence now, but we look forward to the fuller experience that His advent will make possible.

Finding full communion

God has always wanted full communion with us. But allowing Him that freedom doesn't come naturally to us. I remember sitting in my parents' church week after week, deciding I *would* be a Christian. In a mighty effort of willpower, I'd maybe last an hour or two before my insistent conscience would give me notice of something I had just done that wasn't right. And then the dread cloud of despair would creep over me, shutting out God's sunlight of love.

It was just like a story I heard in Bible class. The story went like this: Once upon a time there was a boy named William Stickers. Bill went to church and tried to be good [just like me, I thought]. But he kept on doing naughty things, things that God didn't like [again, just like me]. Then one day he saw a big sign posted on a wall:

BILL STICKERS WILL BE PROSECUTED.

Bill was terrified. Obviously, people had discovered all the bad things he had done. Running home as fast as he could, he shut himself in his room.

When his parents found him, they asked him why he was hiding. At first he didn't want to tell them about his sins and the trial he faced. But finally he told them the whole story. And of course they laughed—because the sign was simply the English equivalent of "Post No Bills." Bill stickers are people who put up unauthorized posters!

All the class laughed at the story—except me. Because I felt just like this apocryphal "Bill Stickers." It took God's dramatic intervention in my hopeless and meaningless life before I could even say to myself, "There must be more to life than this." And it took His continuing intervention to lead me to find meaning. Most of all, God brought about my recovery through giving me hope—His hope, hope that was founded on the kind of person this God of hope is.

Eventually the realization struck me, with as strong an impact as a hammer blow to my head, that this wonderful, loving, caring God wanted a relationship with *me*! This suffering Saviour had come for *me*. Though He had died at my hands, He had risen again to assure *my* resurrection. And He had promised to come again—for *me*!

The God of hope promises to return in all His glory to lead us to the eternal home He has prepared for us. The second advent is the means by which His ultimate desire—and ours—is finally achieved: "God himself will *be with them* and be their God" (Revelation 21:3, emphasis supplied).

Jesus' plan to return for us shows that He really is Immanuel, "God with us"—the God of relationships!

CHAPTER 2

True Beacons of Hope

1 Timothy 1:3-11

"Set the fire burning, Jake. I hear there's a schooner full of gold and silk and rum passing by tonight. Now that'd be a catch! If we could lead them onto Dead Man's Rocks—hey, we'd be rich!"

Busily setting their counterfeit signal beacons, the wreckers strained their eyes into the darkness. Glimmering faintly in the night came the riding lights of the doomed ship. Then, to the sailors' anguish and the wreckers' joy, came the sound of splintering timbers.

"Hey, Jake, we have them! Listen!" And over the crashing of the breakers on the jagged rocks came the cries of drowning men, dying in sight of the shore. "Quick. Call the others. We're going to feast tonight. Kill anyone who's still alive; we don't want this to get out." With a shout of "Let's go," the wreckers slip into the darkness of betrayal.

On Cornwall's rocky coasts, the wreckers of the seventeenth and eighteenth centuries set false lights on the cliff tops to lure passing vessels onto the reefs. Once a ship was aground, these evil men would gather like vultures round a kill, plundering all they could haul ashore. Any survivors were quickly disposed of, since "dead men tell no tales."

What should have been beacons of hope were beguiling lamps of despair, enticing lost sailors to their deaths on the rocks. Each wrecker was a false watchman of the night, leading astray those who were foolish enough to trust the lights of trickery; each was

17

one of those who "kindles on the coast / False fires, that others may be lost" (William Wordsworth).

The world has seen many false fires—beacons that promise safe harbor but instead lead people to shipwreck their faith, that offer hope where none is to be found. The books *Mein Kampf* of Hitler and *Das Kapital* of Marx, the Peruvian revolutionary fighters of the Shining Path and the Maharishi Mahesh Yogi, the Western capitalistic utopias and Jamaican Rastafarianism— all promise a "salvation" either here and now or in the future, and all fail because of the sinfulness of humanity and our inability to save ourselves.

We have "the *truth*"

Misleading "lights" exist within the church as well as outside it. In the letter Paul wrote to Timothy, he warns him about the self-appointed individuals who believe they have a mission to put the church right, to make sure that everyone believes just as they do. "We have the truth," they say. "Don't listen to the pastor. Don't listen to the consensus of the church. Don't listen to anyone but us. *We have the truth!*"

These would-be spiritual lights sit unmoved by appeals to love and fellowship, to the unity of the faith. Faces hard as flint, they are ever ready to defend themselves and their positions, always ready to argue and fight and "discuss" (see 1 Timothy 1:4, 6).

Sometimes, we must admit, some charges leveled against the church may have some truth to them. But possession of "the truth" never justifies un-Christlike words or actions.

I know of one church in which the members fought over the posture people should assume in prayer! Whenever a public prayer was offered, the factions took up the cudgels: some would bow, some would kneel, some would stand. Instead of spending their time talking with God, they spent it fighting each other.

Hats. Veils. Patterned hosiery. Clothing that combined certain colors. Children's use of drawing books in the service. Shaking hands. Ceremonial feast days. Laying on of hands at baptism. Padded kneelers for prayer. The right recipe for communion bread. Even how to park cars in the church parking lot— I have seen churches fight over these and a thousand other topics. The issues are themselves trivial—but the battles they bring, with the resultant pain, hatred, and destruction of spirituality, are to be strongly condemned.

It is precisely because of the carnage these battles cause that Paul writes so strongly to Timothy. Some folk in Ephesus seem to have become fascinated by myths and legends, whether Jewish or Greek or otherwise. Much of what these false teachers were saying must have seemed silly to Paul, and hardly worth the effort of refuting. But because it was hurting the church, he had to say something—and, in fact, gave an order (see 1 Timothy 1:4, 5). Some people, he wrote, had turned away from the love of a pure heart, a clear conscience, and a genuine faith, and "have lost their way in foolish discussions" (1 Timothy 1:6, TEV).

But there is something worse than church members allowing themselves to be distracted by foolish discussions. Something worse than their majoring in minors. *At all costs, the church must avoid giving the wrong impression of God.*

What *kind* of God?

Church members may have the strange experience of finding themselves agreeing with fellow believers on all the points of doctrine and yet disagreeing on the *kind* of person God really is! One may view the day of worship as God's arbitrary test of unquestioning obedience, and the other may consider it God's wonderful provision for help and blessing. The first may regard the second coming as God's dreadful day of vindictive vengeance, while the other sees it as the long-anticipated arrival of her Friend and Saviour. One may say that biblical laws are standards of performance set by a demanding God; the other, that they are the gracious counsel of the caring Creator God.

Perhaps we really do need that very first one of the twenty-seven fundamentals of our faith to outline clearly what God is like! All too frequently a perverse and perverted understanding of God lies at the heart of the trouble churches experience. Take the problem in Ephesus, about which Paul writes to Timothy. Presumably, the "legends and long . . . long lists of ancestors" (verse 4, TEV) refer to attempts to trace their descent. What do these efforts tell us about the Ephesians' view of God? That He exhibits favoritism? The Jews had already expressed that to Jesus, when they arrogantly told Him that they were "Abraham's seed" (see Matthew 3:9). Jesus' reply, that He could raise up children of Abraham from stones, points out the fallibility of their reasoning: It doesn't matter who your parents are; God's love is not conditioned on having the right ancestors.

So then, to say that it *is* directly misrepresents God. To say that someone's ancestry or knowledge of "legends" or speculative "learning" influences God's attitude toward that person adulterates the truth about the God of the gospel, who offers salvation to *all* who will receive Him. That's why this heresy was so dangerous. In place of the good news, it was substituting some speculative teaching that could not save. *Because these misrepresentations threaten some people's salvation, Paul said the truth must be told!*

Why then the law?

Paul warned Timothy about people who, by claiming authority and making spurious appeals to God's law, were leading others away from the gospel. Those who claim to support the law need to remember that "the Law is good *if it is used as it should be used*" (1 Timothy 1:8, TEV, emphasis supplied). It's all too easy to forget the reason why God gave the law. As Paul makes clear to Timothy in the next verse, laws are made for lawbreakers!

So, as Galatians 3:19 asks, "What, then, was the purpose of the law?" Paul's answer: "It was added"—added as a way of defining wrong, added to reveal the sinfulness of sin. But not added to save. As Paul makes so clear, only God can save.

Does observing the law make us good? Apparently the Pharisees believed that it does. In fact, they developed a whole legal system to make sure they wouldn't even *unintentionally* commit a sin. Tragically, for themselves and for everyone who bought into their system of belief, they had misunderstood God. The very ones who thought that by rigid observance and ritual sacrifice they could gain favor with God, ended up killing Him when He came! In the words of William James, "There is no greater lie than a truth misunderstood."

How do people define "being a Christian"? Isn't it usually in terms of doing this or not doing that? We tend to define Christianity in *behavioral* terms instead of seeing it as it truly is: basically *relational.*

Refraining from doing wrong does not make us good. It is our *essence* rather than our *actions* that determines whether or not we are good. I committed no murder, rape, arson, theft, adultery, grand larceny, or high treason today. Does that make me good? If we all were to avoid becoming the kinds of sinners Paul lists in 1 Timothy 1:9, 10, would that be enough? Evidently not; the character Jesus ascribes to His followers in the Sermon on the Mount goes far beyond that.

Chocolate cake

When I was young, I loved chocolate cake. (There are some loves one doesn't outgrow!) The aroma of the cake baking in the oven was enough to bring me running to the kitchen.

One particular day, Mum set a just-baked cake on the windowsill to cool. Knowing my predilections, she gave me strict instructions not even to touch it, let alone take a piece!

When I went outside to play, the sight and scent of that cake drew me like a magnet. And then a debate began:

Maybe a piece has fallen off.

No. Not even a crumb.

Maybe a piece is loose.

No. Nothing.

I would love to have just a little taste.

She said not to touch it.

Maybe I could slice a piece from the side.

No. She'd notice that.

From the top, then.

No—that'd be even more obvious.

Hey, how about from the bottom. What a brilliant idea!

No, she'd still find out. Better not.

About that time, Mum took the cake back inside. Later, she asked if I had refrained from sampling the cake.

"Yes, Mum," I answered. "I didn't even touch it."

"Good boy!"

Good boy? No.

I told her. I told her that I wasn't a good boy because if I could have gotten away with it, I would have taken a piece.

Smiling sadly, she thanked me for being honest. Then she asked me why I had wasted so much time trying to figure out how to get a piece of cake when I could have been playing. Didn't I know we'd be having that cake for supper?

If we don't do what God asks us not to do just because we know we can't get away with it, are we good? Hardly! Goodness is not merely a matter of observing commands. It is the desire of the heart that counts.

Right for right's sake

If we will let Him, God will so change us that sin will become abhorrent to us. We will want to do right simply because it *is* right. For it was not primarily humankind's breaking of laws that brought sin into this world, but their disbelieving, distrusting, disowning God. And it is only as we come to trust God completely that the harmony of the universe can be reestablished. It is only as we enter into a loving relationship with Him that the damages of sin can be repaired and the devil's charges refuted.

For it is the goodness of God that leads us to repentance (see Romans 2:4)—not fear of punishment for the breaking of laws. In fact, fearing God—that is, being frightened of Him because we regard Him as hostile—reveals that we do not have the right relationship with Him. For "there is no fear in love; perfect love drives out all fear. So then, love has not been made perfect in anyone who is afraid, because fear has to do with punishment" (1 John 4:18, TEV). For us to have the right relationship with God, we must know Him as He truly is and agree that His way is unquestionably right.

Flight of anger

On a flight from Dallas–Fort Worth to New York, I was assigned a seat next to a young woman. As we climbed into the sky after takeoff, she picked up a news magazine and started reading. Suddenly she burst out in anger: "I hate all this fighting and killing. Look what they're doing now—murdering innocent babies and children. And what about all these people starving to death. How could there be a God? Kind and loving, they say. Well, look at that!"

Slapping the pictures in the magazine, she launched into a terrible tirade, cataloging the evils and sufferings of this world and running down any 'god' who could allow such things.

Then she turned to me. "What do you think?"

"Yes, I'm sure you're right," I told her.

We talked for a while. Then she asked, "By the way, what do you do?"

"I'm a minister."

She was surprised, embarrassed, and confused all at once. "I'm sorry. I didn't mean . . . But how come you agreed with me?"

For the next four hours we talked about God. About what He's like. About the challenges of Satan's rebellion. About God's need to *demonstrate* His true nature, rather than simply make claims. About the sinfulness of sin, and what it leads to. About God's valuing of our freedom to choose. About all the issues in the great controversy over God's character and government.

Just before we parted, she said quietly, "I never before saw God as good."

The gospel is the *good* news of a *good* God; it's the good news of what He has done for us, what He will do for us.

Only "fraud and falsehood . . . dread examination. Truth invites it" (Thomas Cooper); "Who speaks the truth stabs falsehood in the heart" (James Russell Lowell).

Our mission is to be beacons of hope, revealing to the world the truth of the goodness of God. We must outshine the beguiling beacons of delusions lighted by those who speak falsely.

We need to tell the truth about God, "that teaching [of sound doctrine] is found in the gospel that was entrusted me to announce, the Good News from the glorious and blessed God" (1 Timothy 1:11, TEV).

CHAPTER 3

Sin Healing

7/25

1 Timothy 1:12-20

"Roll up, roll up! Dr. Brown's miraculous elixir of incredible potency is yours—yes, yours—for just ten cents a bottle. Watch the years just melt away! Feel that terrible pain ease away in moments! Experience the bliss of having your ailments, no matter what they are, cured!"

That speech, or one similar, has always found an audience. From the mystic incantations and "natural" remedies of the past to the advertising hype and wonder-drug cures of the present, how little has changed! The charlatans are still peddling their bogus wares. Whether the "magic ingredient" is shark oil or "Special Formula X," someone, somewhere, will believe it will work—or at least that it's worth a try.

Fake cures. Quack doctors. Medical charlatans. Feeding on men and women desperate enough to try anything that might remedy their ills, even though some of the supposed "cures" might be lethal!

Joshua Ward, who operated in England in the eighteenth century, grew rich on his two products: "the pill" and "the drop." Both were made from antimony compounds that could kill, yet he was highly regarded and even served King George II.

Count Alessandro Cagliostro from Palermo, Italy, was an even more famous "physician" contemporary with Ward. He claimed both to be an alchemist and to possess magical powers that he used in formulating his compounds: restoratives, elixirs of life, and a special potion for making ugly women beautiful! Always suave and sophisticated, his business empire flourished despite his being imprisoned in France, England, and Italy at various times. He died a rich man in 1795.

Fake cures for the ravages of disease. False hope for the despairing. Deceitful promises, straws useless to those who were drowning in an ocean of sickness. Yet the greater evil and the worse deceit are the supposed cures charlatans offer for *spiritual* sickness. These swindlers play on people's spiritual gullibility, fooling them into trusting that which cannot save, believing in that which cannot heal.

Where, then, can we find dependable remedies for the sin that troubles us? Before we can find a cure, we need to make a diagnosis, to discover the origin of the problem. You can't make something right without knowing what went wrong! As Søren Kierkegaard said, "Christianity begins with the doctrine of sin."

What is sin?

What, then, is sin? The Bible gives us some clear definitions:

"Everyone who sins breaks the law; in fact, sin is lawlessness" (1 John 3:4).

"All wrongdoing is sin" (1 John 5:17).

"Anyone, then, who knows the good he ought to do and doesn't do it, sins" (James 4:17).

"Whatsoever is not of faith is sin" (Romans 14:23, KJV).

Let's look a little more closely at what the Bible is saying here. First John 3:4 says, "Sin is the transgression of the law" (KJV). Is the Bible suggesting that we sin only when we deliberately break the law? Clearly not: Paul reminds us that sin remains sin even though we may not be aware of it (see Romans 7). So sin is not just a conscious breaking of some known law. We may well be transgressing laws we don't even know about—and our ignorance does not excuse us.

Well, what if we live absolutely exemplary lives; what if, like the Pharisees, we are careful to observe each law in minute detail—will that render us acceptable to God? No. The mere absence of infractions of specific statutes does not make us good. Before Paul's conversion, this realization troubled him. His great religious zeal, which drove him to prove his faithfulness through persecuting Christians, offered his sin-sick soul no succor.

Sin is no mere action or lack of action. Sin lies at the very heart of our being. And because sin is such an integral part of our being, we often fail to understand it.

So how do we come to grips with it? How can we understand what it involves?

I once saw a billboard advertising a movie. The slogan read: CRIME IS A DISEASE. MEET THE CURE.

The cure was Sylvester Stallone in one of his guises, offering a very physical response to crime—not very helpful as an answer to the sin problem! But that slogan, somewhat altered, offers a good perspective on both what sin is and how we may find help with it:

SIN IS A DISEASE. MEET THE CURE—JESUS.

The cure for lawlessness

We've come a little closer to answering our question as to what sin is. The New International Version's translation of 1 John 3:4 adds further enlightenment: "Sin is lawlessness."

For many people, the word *lawlessness* brings to mind stereotyped images of the old American West: Outlaws. Lawless frontier towns. Bandits. The only "law" of the land, the law of the gun.

Of course, this may largely be a myth perpetuated by TV and novel, but if the people of that time and place were lawless, why were they? Was it because they spent their time breaking the law? Or was it rather because of their attitude? *Lawlessness* speaks of a way of thinking and living that is out of harmony with the standard of conduct that the law expresses. Sin and evil are outworkings of a principle at war with the great law of love and trust that is the foundation of the divine government.

When I was at school, one common winter activity our teachers substituted for organized sports was the cross-country run. They gave us strict instructions as to the route we were to take and what would happen if we "bunked off" or hitched a ride or took a shortcut. This was "the Law."

As we students went out the school gates, we talked a lot about how we could avoid the pain and discomfort of a long, wet, cold, and muddy run. We dreamed up many schemes for outwitting the teachers. Most of us would have willingly broken "the Law." But we didn't. Why not? Because we were afraid of getting caught. We didn't want the punishment. We knew what penalties the teachers would impose on our law-breaking.

Were we good boys? Were we trustworthy and right? Not in the least—we *wanted* to break the law.

Many of us try to live like that, try to avoid active sin because we fear punishment. Perhaps that's a starting point, but it clearly shows that we are still lawless. We still *want* to sin, to live contrary to God's will.

So sin is like a dread disease, a spiritual disease that consists of more than just the symptoms—our actions. Sin poisons the very wellsprings of our lives. It severs us from the life of God; its prognosis is eternal death.

Another Bible definition can increase our understanding of sin: "Whatsoever is not of faith is sin" (Romans 14:23, KJV). At first this text may seem hard to understand. But when you think about it, it's not so difficult. What is faith? It's trusting God, having confidence in Him. So what is the opposite of faith? *Distrust*, not having confidence in God. By this definition, *sin is distrusting God.* Not trusting God to work in one's life. Not believing what He says.

Question: What was Eve's first sin? Was it taking and eating the fruit? Or was it trusting the devil's "Ye shall not surely die" rather than God's warning? The very heart of sin consists of this distrust of God, this suspicion of Him. It's an attitude that says: "God, I may believe You exist. I may even come to church regularly and profess to be a good Christian. But I don't really want Your help; I don't trust You with my life; I don't accept Your healing, saving offer."

The universality of human sinfulness

To complete our understanding of sin and its effect on our world, we must realize that it infects every one of us. The Bible makes this abundantly clear:

"There is no one who does not sin" (1 Kings 8:46).

"Who can say, I have made my heart clean, I am pure from my sin?" (Proverbs 20:9, KJV).

"Everyone has turned away, they have together become corrupt; there is no one that does good, not even one" (Psalm 53:3).

"We all, like sheep, have gone astray, each of us has turned to his own way" (Isaiah 53:6).

"All of us have become like one who is unclean, and all our righteous acts are like filthy rags; we all shrivel up like a leaf, and like the wind our sins sweep us away" (Isaiah 64:6).

"All have sinned, and come short of the glory of God" (Romans 3:23, KJV).

"If we say that we have no sin, we deceive ourselves, and the truth is not in us" (1 John 1:8, KJV).

Carrying the idea of sin as a disease a little further, would it make sense for a doctor to say to his sick patient: "I diagnose you as suffering from this particular disease. I therefore propose to penalize you for this. The penalty will be . . ."? Of course not! Sin brings its own natural and painful consequences. John Boys said, "Sin is the great punishment of sin."

In fact, God condemns sin in part because it is death to us: "Sin is not hurtful because it is forbidden, but it is forbidden because it is hurtful" (Franklin). These results are inherent in sin itself; ultimately, sin is self-destructive:

"Evil shall slay the wicked: and they that hate the righteous shall be desolate" (Psalm 34:21, KJV).

"He that sinneth against me wrongeth his own soul: all they that hate me love death" (Proverbs 8:36, KJV).

"People who can't be trusted are destroyed by their own dishonesty" (Proverbs 11:3, TEV).

"The look on their faces testifies against them; they parade their sin like Sodom; they do not hide it. Woe to them! They have brought disaster upon themselves" (Isaiah 3:9).

"O Israel, thou hast destroyed thyself" (Hosea 13:9, KJV).

"Sin pays its wage—death" (Romans 6:23, TEV).

"They . . . shall utterly perish in their own corruption" (2 Peter 2:12, KJV).

The result is that "the sinner sins against himself; the wrong-

doer wrongs himself, becoming the worse by his own actions"
(Marcus Aurelius).

Paul, the patient

Paul saw this clearly in his own life. Describing himself as a
blasphemer, a persecutor, and a violent man (see 1 Timothy
1:13), he called himself "the worst of sinners" (1 Timothy 1:16).
Then he met the loving, healing God who wanted to save him
from himself. Years later this experience still overwhelmed
him. He described it to Timothy: "Christ Jesus came into the
world to save sinners. I am the worst of them, but God was
merciful to me in order that Christ Jesus might show his full
patience in dealing with me, the worst of sinners, as an example
for all those who would later believe in him and receive eternal
life. To the eternal King, immortal and invisible, the only God—
to him be honor and glory forever and ever! Amen" (1 Timothy
1:15-17, TEV).

The worst of sinners! For Paul, the depth of his sinfulness
multiplied his thankfulness for God's grace. Understanding
where the road he had been on was taking him increased Paul's
amazement at God's incredible offer of healing salvation. Paul
had tried the false cures of legalism, the pseudohealing that
ritual observance vainly promised, and had not found the inner
peace or the healing of his sin-sickness for which his heart
ached.

The worst of sinners—like us. For, like Paul, we are *sin
addicts*, drugged by our own actions and unable to stop ourselves:

Humanity takes "pleasure in sin" (2 Thessalonians 2:12, TEV),
"drinks evil as if it were water" (Job 15:16, TEV). We are people
"who delight in doing wrong, who have joy in wilful wickedness"
(Proverbs 2:14, Moffatt); for we "love evil rather than good, falsehood rather than speaking the truth" (Psalm 52:3).

We have gone away from God, built a barricade between us
and Him, and, like spoiled children, refuse to come back to the
only One who can heal us from the deadly leprosy of sin. But God
has broken through that barricade. He comes to us asking us to
allow Him to make us whole again.

Treatment

My son Paul had a bad fall when he was about two years old. He cut his head open to the bone. He was in trouble—he was sick, if you like. At any rate he had a bad "health problem."

Now he could have said: "I know I'm in trouble. I know I'm hurt and need immediate attention. But I just don't trust you, Mum and Dad. I don't trust the surgeon to repair the damage done. I'm just going to live as I want and do as I think best."

That would have been ridiculous, wouldn't it? Obviously, he needed immediate treatment. When it comes to sin, we do too.

Now imagine that Paul goes off to the hospital for treatment. The kind doctor comes out to see him, and says, "Oh my, you have got yourself into trouble, haven't you? You have been naughty. And you got into trouble because of doing things you shouldn't. But that's all right. I forgive you." And then the doctor disappears back inside his office.

That would be just as foolish. While we seek God's forgiveness for the wrongs we have *done*, that doesn't remove the wrong that we *are*. Often we fail to see the sinfulness of sin. We are spiritually shortsighted, not understanding what the breaking of our relationship with our heavenly Father really means. Truly, "our sense of sin is in proportion to our nearness to God" (Thomas D. Bernard). In the words of J. C. Ryle, "I am convinced that the first step towards attaining a higher standard of holiness is to realize more fully the amazing sinfulness of sin."

Sin is a spiritual disease, a disease of distrusting God. And only God can be the cure. *We need to meet the cure.* Only God can win us back to love Him and trust Him. We cannot do this by ourselves any more than disease-ravaged patients can cure themselves.

"Therefore, if anyone is in Christ, he is a new creation; the old has gone, the new has come!" (2 Corinthians 5:17). When we are in Christ, we don't live for ourselves anymore. Our loving God will change that spirit of self-centered rebellion, if we will let Him. He will create us anew. He reconciles us to Him, not counting our sinful predispositions against us.

Just as a doctor doesn't hold a patient's disease against the patient, God doesn't hold the sin disease against us. He doesn't intend for us to *remain* diseased, of course. He intends healing us, curing us. "In him we [can] *become* the righteousness of God" (2 Corinthians 5:21). *Become.* Not have, but in some way *be* God's righteousness. We become His demonstration of what He can do, how He can change sin-diseased humanity.

Coming home

I remember running away from home when I was about five. I've forgotten what the problem was—I was mad about something and didn't want to stay with my parents. Anyway, I went upstairs and packed my case. I was leaving home.

I decided to make my new home in the garden shed. Now, I knew it wasn't well furnished; it was cold and drafty and the roof leaked. There was no food there, no toys, and I was completely alone in the dark. But I was by myself.

It didn't take me long to realize that I was being very stupid. I wanted to go back home. I missed my nice warm bed. I missed a good meal on the table. I missed my toys and books. But most of all, I missed my family. I wanted to go home, but I couldn't.

Thankfully, it didn't take long for my mother to come to the shed and say, "Jonathan, supper's ready. Are you coming in?"

No criticism from her. No arguments. Just a warm, loving acceptance.

That's our God. He comes to us and graciously invites us back, showing what He's really like. Paul described his experience of God's grace to Timothy: Our Lord "poured out his grace upon me, giving me tremendous faith in, and love for, himself. . . . It was a kind of demonstration of the extent of Christ's patience toward the worst of men, to serve as an example to all who in the future should trust him for eternal life" (1 Timothy 1:14-16, Phillips).

Spiritual charlatans abound. But "why spend money on what is not bread, and your labor on what does not satisify?" asks God (Isaiah 55:2). In effect, "Why go to those who can't help you? Come to Me!"

Sin is a disease. Meet the cure: God Himself.

CHAPTER 4

7/26

True Worship

1 Timothy 2

Tarim was up well before dawn.

So was the documentary film crew. "Watch how he prepares his offerings with loving care, making sure that all is done properly to express his complete devotion," intoned the interviewer.

"Why do you do this?" asked the interviewer, getting in the way of what Tarim was doing.

"Because this is our custom. It must be done right—otherwise our god will be offended."

The cameraman recorded each intricate step of the ritual. The bowing, the muttered prayers, the ceremonial washing.

"What is the purpose of this? And this?" The interviewer pointed at Tarim's tools and utensils and odd-looking substances. He seemed anxious to understand.

"This is the way it has always been. My father followed this way, and his father before him." Tarim went on plaiting the vines, marking the ground, stirring the carefully prepared food. Every once in a while he paused and made strange, solemn gestures.

"What is the meaning of the moves you make?"

"They are part of the ceremony."

Finally Tarim stood. "It is ready," he announced. He picked up his wicker basket, put all the things inside, and walked toward the cliff. The documentary team followed, filming as they went.

At the edge of the cliff, looking down at the gray-green ocean below, Tarim stood with his arms outstretched, eyes closed. He remained still for several minutes and then stepped back.

From his basket Tarim took a large conch shell. He blew three short blasts, and then one long one.

"I think this is to summon the god's spirit," commented the interviewer.

Then Tarim poured water out over the edge of the cliff.

"This must be to bathe the god and give him something to refresh him."

Tarim pulled out a dish of specially prepared food and threw it in a high arc out over the abyss.

"I believe he is now making his food offering to please the god. This must be the central part of this worship ceremony." The interviewer sounded very intense.

Finally, Tarim spread the net of plaited vines on the cliff edge and chanted some strange words. "Obviously asking for help in his next catch. A prayer of devotion and dedication," the interviewer added.

Then Tarim left. He was smiling. And as he walked back down the path, he chuckled to himself.

"Imagine. They were even bigger fools than I thought. They really did believe that all my nonsense was worship of some god! As if all that posturing and ceremony would make any difference to my catch! All I need are my nylon nets, my outboard engine, and my fiberglass boat. Worship? What a joke!"

Cynics or fools?

What about us? Are we cynics like Tarim or susceptible, gullible, unquestioning fools like the documentary team? The real truth about worship fits neither of these categories!

But most people have no real understanding of what worship is. To someone looking in from the outside, it may well appear baffling and bewildering.

People use the term *hocus pocus* as some magic spell when doing conjuring tricks or when describing some devious trickery. What many don't realize is that this mysterious incantation actually came from Christian worship—in fact, from the mass.

When the priest intoned over the bread "This is my body," the Latin words he actually said were *Hoc est corpus meum.*" But the common people heard it as "Hocus pocus"! Misunderstanding this incantation that supposedly turned the bread into Christ's body, they thought it a magical charm or spell.

But even for those who understand the words, worship is not an easy idea. It can be both hard to describe and hard to do—so the question: How do I worship?

In 1 Timothy 2, Paul asks Timothy to think of certain elements of worship, including prayer, praise, thanksgiving, modesty, respect, and, above all, preaching and teaching. His request indicates that worship must have content. It is not enough just to go through rituals—worship must be an expression of the believer's thoughts about God and to God.

That's why Paul also writes, "I urge you, brothers, in view of God's mercy, to offer your bodies as living sacrifices, holy and pleasing to God—which is your spiritual worship" (Romans 12:1).

Our worship to God involves our very lives. It's not just something we do once a week in church services. *Worship reflects who we are and whose we are.*

Consequently, the exact format of worship can never be set in concrete. By its very definition, worship cannot be limited to certain activities, for "in true worship men . . . have little thought of the means of worship; their thoughts are upon God. True worship is characterized by self-effacement and is lacking in any self-consciousness" (Geoffrey Thomas).

For too many, worship requires no thought. It is simply some kind of required rite, something that is "done."

"We had worship."

"I went to worship."

"College worships are mandatory."

As if worship was some object, some *thing* instead of the reflection of our awe and praise for the relationship God has invited us to have with Him! "Carnal men are content with the 'act' of worship; they have no desire for communion with God" (John W. Everett).

Yes—you can attend a worship service and not think of

worship, not participate in it. As Jesus said, "God is Spirit, and only by the power of his Spirit can people worship him as he really is" (John 4:24, TEV). When people are too busy acting out the acts and never thinking of the meaning and purpose of what they are saying or doing, their worship is the vain worship, the uninformed worship, that Jesus rejected (see Mark 7:7; John 4:22).

What is worship?

J. Oswald Saunders defined worship as "the adoring contemplation of God as He has revealed Himself in Christ and in His Word." Austin Phelps noted that "in the most lofty devotion we become unconscious of self." Romans 12:1 tells us that true worship is our offering of ourselves to God, so that we can truly be "dedicated to his service and pleasing to him" (TEV).

Worship, then, is the ongoing expression of delight in God that is part of the divine-human relationship that Jesus came to restore. We can accept it and enter into that marvelous attitude of prayerful praise, of adoring wonder, of trusting assurance—or we can stand outside and criticize and complain. But we must remember that "a man can no more diminish God's glory by refusing to worship Him than a lunatic can put out the sun by scribbling the word 'darkness' on the walls of his cell" (C. S. Lewis).

The comments about the role of women, exact dress requirements, and ornamentation that Paul makes in 1 Timothy 2 are side issues. They are not to be taken as the most important aspects of worship. Paul doesn't want the believers in Ephesus to major in minors, but to act wisely and practically. The heart of his message is: "There is one God, and there is one who brings God and mankind together, the man Christ Jesus, who gave himself to redeem mankind" (1 Timothy 2:5, 6, TEV). Paul says what he does about these side issues simply because he does not want those who worship to be distracted!

For the distractions of this world are very insistent and very real. It is easy to become so involved in all the trivial details of life that we miss the important themes and objectives—like the rich fool who spent all his life amassing *things* and yet was not rich toward God (see Luke 12:16-21). We get wrapped up in the bits and pieces of life, not the whole. The nuts and bolts of a person, not the complete being. The jigsaw pieces with their funny shapes, and not the beautiful picture they make.

The trivia of life.

Trivial because these bits and pieces of life we get so wrapped up in make us lose sight of who we are, where we're going, and what it all means. Such preoccupation with the inconsequential can affect us all.

Look at Solomon's testimony in Ecclesiastes 2. Immersing himself in all kinds of activities, he experimented with all that life could offer—trying to see what meaning there was "under the sun." His tragic conclusion: "Then I thought about all that I had done and how hard I had worked doing it, and I realized that it didn't mean a thing. It was like chasing the wind—of no use at all" (Ecclesiastes 2:11, TEV).

Forgetting God

What with all the business—read "busy-ness"—of life, it's all too easy to forget why we do what we do. Christians study the things of God—and are tempted to stay on that level: merely studying the *things* of God. We become so involved in studying *about* God that we forget the reason we started studying in the first place.

With so much to do and so much to learn and so much to say, the danger is, as Robert Frost suggested, that we spend our lives doing "a little bit of everything / A great deal of none."

Triviality—the way of busy forgetfulness. Where is our relationship to God in all of this? Where is our worship? Where is the remembered reverence of "the one who brings God and mankind together, the man Christ Jesus?" (see 1 Timothy 2:5).

"Come on," someone says. "We've got to be practical. We can't spend our lives dreaming and mooning about looking for the lost chord or something. We've got to get on with the business of living and not get bogged down worrying about all these 'higher things.'

"When do I have time for anything more than getting assignments in on time or getting to work or arranging a date or organizing meetings? Then there's my hobby and family time and church duties and . . . and . . . With all I have to do, where can I find time to think about such abstract matters as the 'meaning of life'? We've got to be practical.

"Worship? Oh yes, I do that! What do you mean, I have to *think* about it? Come on, get real!"

And so we throw ourselves into the frenzied rush of what we call our lives, and before we know it, our time is up! "The world is too much with us: late and soon, / Getting and spending, we lay waste our powers" (William Wordsworth).

We turn ourselves into "people-machines," churning out work without thought, products without reason—whether they be plastic cups in a factory or dissertations in a seminary. We become, in the words of Thomas Hardy, part of "the monotonous moils of strained, hard-run humanity."

So, by occupying ourselves with trivia in our pursuit of happiness, we destroy ourselves. Out of harmony with time, we are not really living. And not only are we out of harmony with time, we are also *out* of time—time runs out on us, leaving us clutching a handful of straw that we thought was a bunch of roses.

In addition, we are out of harmony with reality. As Jesus put it: "They seeing see not; and hearing they hear not, neither do they understand" (Matthew 13:13, KJV).

And here a particular danger threatens. For the trivia of religion can as certainly sidetrack us as can any other trivia—it obscures and demeans the brightness of truth it was meant to illuminate. Argued doctrine and defended dogma can crush the innocent vision of youth, the childlike trust and belief in the actual presence of God. If anything so overwhelms us that we forget why we are here, that we forget the reality of God, then our lives are trivial.

Yes, we are often in the rut because we were pushed there. Yes, we do have responsibilities. Yes, we do at times need to be practical. *But we do not have to be satisfied with life's trivia.* Worship reminds us that life means more than all these trifles.

By involving ourselves too much with life's bits and pieces, we lay waste our spiritual powers. We lose sight of what is really real. We lose sight of ourselves. We lose sight of God. As trivialized beings, we forget about the God we claim to know as a friend,

and worship becomes a monotonous routine. We travel down the
practical road to ruin.

So what shall we do?

Shall we do something about this situation? Perhaps we don't
even see the necessity of doing anything—all the common tasks
may have blinded us to our predicament. So many people are not
even aware that there is anything beyond the trivia.

> Earth's crammed with heaven,
>   And every common bush afire with God;
> But only he who sees, takes off his shoes,
> The rest sit round it and pluck blackberries.
>   —*Elizabeth Barrett Browning*

I especially like that last line. It sums up this unseeing
preoccupation with the mundane things of life, the trivia of
existence that blinds the eye to what really matters. So we must
first look at our lives and acknowledge the problem.

And when we see the trivia of life for what it is, what is the
answer? What is the answer to the forgetfulness, the escapism,
and the pragmatism that triviality brings?

The answer is finding that time, that true spiritual worship
time—whenever that may be. Time when we can leave all this
meaninglessness behind. For we all desperately need time we
share only with God. We need time to work out what everything
means, what is really important and what is not.

We need to see the trivia for what it really is. We need to see
every common bush afire with God. We need to see that "the
world is charged with the grandeur of God" (Gerard Manley
Hopkins). Through all the insignificant bits of our lives, we need
to catch a vision of God.

Like Elisha's servant, we need to see God's chariots all around
us. And only God can provide that vision for us. Only He can
make us see, among all the necessary trivia, the important,
meaningful, fundamental matters that lead us to Him.

I don't often quote the Apocrypha, but there's a line in
2 Esdras 14:25 that's relevant here. It pictures God as saying,

"I shall light a candle of understanding in your heart."

We need that candle of understanding if we are to escape the tyranny of triviality. We need to catch the light that will make dark things plainer—that seeing, we shall see, and hearing, we shall hear *and understand!*

And how may we allow God to light that candle for us? By taking time out of life's repetition. By not just living to live, but asking *Why?* By coming to the author of Truth for help in finding the sense in the senseless.

All things will continue as they were unless . . .

Unless we allow our lives to be crammed with heaven and afire with God. That is what true, living, relational worship is all about.

Utopia?

Sometimes in our searching for a better way of living, we dream of an idyllic place where we can find God and worship Him in spirit and in truth. Hemmed in by all the fussing and fighting of this modern world, some remote utopia attracts us.

Harry Little wanted to find a place that would make that kind of life a reality—at least for himself. So he moved to Mexico and lived there as simply as he could. But before long the pressures of the civilization he had rejected came too close, and so he moved again.

With his blind, deaf wife Jan and his stepdaughter Rebecca, Harry journeyed some sixteen hundred miles up the Amazon. Near the Venezuelan border, he cleared a patch of rain forest and built a thatched house. The dream was coming true; he and his family were alone in the jungle—his nearest neighbors were a six-day boat ride downriver.

Four and a half years later, Harry's utopia—his place to practice "essential" Christianity—had become a rain-drenched hell. The apparently fertile forest covered a desperately poor soil. His family's hope to become self-sufficient receded day by day, and the horrors of their position became increasingly clear. On Christmas 1979, they all became ill. Rebecca died within a few days, and after another month or so of suffering, Harry also died.

Jan survived the fever, but was left alone in the forest—blind and deaf. By a miracle, she was still alive three months later when she was found and rescued.

Like Harry and his family, monks and nuns have tried to separate themselves from the world; dreamers and visionaries have traveled to remote places; Celtic "saints" have sailed in tiny coracles to live in complete isolation on offshore islands. But no special place is required for worshiping God. The burning bush was special only because God was there; the ground was holy only because of His presence. True spiritual worship depends only on our relationship with Him, not on our location—whether that be church or temple or shrine.

Worship comes when our relationship with God is characterized by love and praise and happiness. Worship is giving "worthship"—acknowledging the worth of God as our true Saviour and Friend, Almighty God and Everlasting Father, the Prince of Peace.

Have you come to the place where you agree with the Preacher that "all things are wearisome, more than one can say. The eye never has enough of seeing, or the ear its fill of hearing"; that "all man's efforts are for his mouth, yet his appetite is never satisfied. . . . This too is meaningless, a chasing after the wind" (Ecclesiastes 1:8; 6:7, 9, KJV)?

If so, then go to God. Quietly, in private, ask Him to liberate you from all the trivialities of your life and to show you His meaning and purpose *for you*. "He reveals the deep and secret things" (Daniel 2:22, KJV).

When life's triviality threatens to overwhelm you, reach for the antidote: the assurance of God in your life—now and always—through your quiet times alone with your Maker and Remaker, the Creator of all that is good and true, the Filler of empty hearts, and the Conqueror of all meaningless trivia. The God "who wants everyone to be saved and to come to know the truth" (1 Timothy 2:4, TEV). The God of true, spiritual worship.

Be Thou my vision O Lord of my heart;
Naught be all else to me, save that Thou art—
Thou my best thought, by day or by night,
Waking or sleeping, Thy presence my light.—Mary E. Byrne.

CHAPTER 5

7/27

The Character of Christian Leadership

1 Timothy 3

A strange statue stands in the cathedral at Toledo, Spain. It is a representation of a dark-skinned Moorish leader. Originally from North Africa, the Moors were Muslims who invaded and ruled Spain from the eighth century on. Why is this "enemy"—who was both an invader and an infidel—remembered in this way?

In 1085, the Moors and King Alfonso VI of Spain—who had fought each other in many battles—signed a treaty that ceded the city of Toledo to the Spanish. The treaty provided, however, for those Moors who remained in Toledo to go on practicing their religion.

But the thought of these non-Christians being allowed to worship angered the local bishop. While the king was traveling, the bishop persuaded the queen to renege on this provision of the treaty, arguing that agreements made with heretics need not be kept.

When the king returned, he found soldiers stationed at the mosque to prevent anyone entering. Furious with the bishop, the king sentenced him to death by burning for daring to contradict his command.

Hearing of this, Abu Walid, the Moorish leader, came to the king and pleaded for the bishop's life. Amazed at the compassion this supposed enemy and infidel showed, the king granted Abu Walid's request, sparing the bishop's life.

And when a new cathedral was built in Toledo, Abu Walid's true spirit of kindness and dramatic intervention were remembered, and a statue made to commemorate this chivalrous man. Abu Walid demonstrated the essence of love to a Christian who acted like an infidel.

An honorable ambition

"This is a true saying: If a man is eager to be a church leader, he desires an excellent work. A church leader must be without fault; he must have only one wife, be sober, self-controlled, and orderly; he must welcome strangers in his home; he must be able to teach; he must not be a drunkard or a violent man, but gentle and peaceful; he must not love money; he must be able to manage his own family well and make his children obey him with all respect" (1 Timothy 3:1-4, TEV).

Within the church there is much scope for the misuse of power. And since abuses are less expected there, they are often harder to deal with. When evil is done from "religious principles"—as the bishop of Toledo did—then great harm can result. Aspiring to leadership is "an honourable ambition" (1 Timothy 3:1, NEB). But the church needs to ensure that those who serve as leaders rightly reflect the God whom they claim to honor.

The church is judged by its membership, and especially by its leadership. That's why Paul specifies the qualities of Christian leaders so carefully. Rightly representing God is the real issue here. The church leader "must not be a beginner in the faith, for fear of his becoming conceited and sharing Satan's downfall. He should, in addition to the above qualifications, have a good reputation with the outside world" (1 Timothy 3:6, 7, Phillips).

At the heart of the matter is the continuation of the great controversy over God's nature and character. God is answering the devil's charges; His answers come in His dealings with all His Creation, including us. And that is why the failures of church leadership don't inflict damage only on a church or on Christian individuals. Such failures reflect on God—for the community of believers is "God's household" (1 Timothy 3:15, TEV).

So what are Christian leaders to demonstrate? Napoleon said,

"A leader is a dealer in hope." This description certainly fits the Christian leader who is motivated by the hope of eternal life. That must have been particularly true when Paul was writing to Timothy, for at that time the church was a persecuted sect. Church leadership was nothing to boast about. It could get a person killed—and often did! Leaders of the early church were most certainly dealers in hope; they promoted the only hope that was of any real relevance—the only true and blessed hope. And the hope they ardently grasped and championed was founded on the God of hope!

Christian leaders are no mere "vain speakers" either. Paul would have agreed that "leadership is action, not position" (Donald McGannon). They lead from the front—not like the mythical general who "led" his army into battle from the rear so that he would be in the right position to lead the retreat!

Paul wanted leaders who were wise and totally committed. He wanted those who were of good character and sincere (see 1 Timothy 3:8, TEV). And while, as Tacitus said, reason and judgment are qualities important to leadership, Paul stresses example most strongly. In contrast, all too often this world's leaders seem to ask people to do as they say, not as they do.

The best kind of leadership

The best kind of leadership is leadership by example.

For more than forty years Sir Wilfred Grenfell worked among the Eskimo people of Labrador. His loving dedication to meeting their dire needs won their hearts. Through working to alleviate their poverty and to provide some basic medical care, he preached the gospel in a highly practical way. By the time of his death, he had founded six hospitals and seven nursing stations along the Labrador coast.

In 1927 King George V presented Grenfell with the Livingstone Gold Medal. Yet Grenfell's satisfaction was not in such marks of approval but in the service he was able to do and in "feeling the nearness of God's presence" as he traveled by sleigh through the snow. His hope of eternal life was strong; to him it seemed as if it "lay just over the horizon of ice, in the eternal blue beyond."

A member of Parliament from the age of twenty-one, William Wilberforce dedicated his life to the abolition of slavery in the British Empire. Influenced by John Newton, the former slave-ship captain, Wilberforce worked tirelessly through the years to move Parliament to act against the slave trade—even though British business was heavily dependent on this lucrative trade.

In 1807 a bill was passed that began the process. Slavery itself was not abolished until 1833; Wilberforce gave his last public speech to urge the passage of the bill that would accomplish that end. He died shortly afterward. The following year, 800,000 slaves received their freedom as the result of Wilberforce's campaign. He was buried among the great in Westminster Abbey. Wilberforce did his work, not for the fame it brought him, but for the glory of *God*.

John Groom was appalled by the conditions of the flower girls that he saw on his way to work in London. Many of them crippled, they eked out a miserable existence selling flowers or bunches of watercress to the passersby who would buy them. When Groom was asked to be the superintendent of a Christian mission, he hired premises near the flower market and brought the girls there for bread and cocoa. As they warmed up in the heated room, he would read Bible stories to them.

After a while he decided to make the mission into a place where the girls could work for wages. He supplied fabric from which they made flowers that could then be sold at a profit. In this way he financed homes for the girls and provided for their daily needs. Groom demonstrated his Christian concern in very practical terms.

These were true Christian leaders, men who used their positions to benefit those who could not help themselves. Truly, actions speak much louder than words.

Speaking good of God

But while actions speak louder than words, we still need to speak for God verbally. How are we to do it? How do Christians "speak boldly about their faith in Christ Jesus" (1 Timothy 3:13, TEV)? How are we to represent Him—especially as leaders? (And we are all leaders of one kind or another; the words of 1 Timothy

3 are not just for elders and deacons—they apply to every member of the church.)

Well, how do you compliment people? If I were to tell you about an old friend of mine—if I were to say that I trust him, that he has these certain abilities, that I count him one of my closest friends, that I admire and respect him—how would you feel about him? Would what I had said make you want to get to know him too?

It's certainly good to compliment people—if the compliments are true. But saying good things you don't mean about someone is damaging. And saying nice things we don't mean about God is just as damaging. Nobody wants to hear that sort of thing, least of all God.

So in speaking for God, point one is that we must mean what we say and say only what we mean.

Point two is that it's hard to say good things about a person one doesn't know. If I don't know God, I can't talk knowledgeably about Him. If I try, my words will sound hollow and empty because they're not based on personal experience.

Third, if you're witnessing only because you feel it's your duty to witness or your minister told you that you should or it seems to be something a Christian has to do—*then please don't do it!* Because you can't say anything good about God to someone else if you don't really want to say it! If it's a burden, if you hate it— then people will notice. To witness effectively, you must *want* to say good things about God.

Presuming, then, that we know God and want to share Him with others, where are we to begin? I believe the very best place is where God showed Himself most clearly—in Jesus.

Tell me, why did Jesus come to this earth? Jesus Himself gave the reason: "In fact, for this reason I was born, and for this I came into the world, *to testify to the truth*" (John 18:37, emphasis supplied).

The devil "is a liar and the father of lies" (John 8:44). Jesus came to show that what the devil said was a lie and that what God said was the truth. The only way God could prove His case was to come Himself—so that everybody could see! And if we are trying to make this God known, we must reveal Him in Jesus.

For, "no one has ever seen God, but God the only Son, who is at the Father's side, has made him known" (John 1:18).

Making God known

How did Jesus accomplish this? How did He make God known? Think with me for a moment. How did Jesus come? As a baby. Not with great wealth, power, or position. But as the child of some poor peasant family in a far-off corner of the Roman Empire.

How did He grow up? Just like the vast majority of human beings—without the benefit of an advanced education, without a lot of personal possessions. He knew what it meant to work hard to earn His food, living just like so many others.

How did He begin His ministry? By being baptized like us— even though He had no need to repent of anything!

Then think of how He made God known in His first miracle. Turning water into wine at the wedding was a perfect demonstration of God's generous and transforming attitude.

Think of how He healed thousands upon thousands—miracles upon miracles to show that God wants us to be well, physically and spiritually; that He does not cause pain and suffering, disease and death. Above all, the gifts of healing, feeding, and caring that He gave showed the love of God in a dramatic way.

Think of how He spoke. He didn't use elaborate or emotionally manipulative oratory. Rather, firmly and lovingly, He showed people the way back to their caring Lord. His parables—above all the one picturing the weeping, loving father welcoming home his prodigal son—say, "That's God."

Jesus lived as God among us—Emmanuel. That's why He said, "If you really knew me, you would know my Father as well. From now on, you do know him and have seen him" (John 14:7). *If you know Jesus, you know God.* Simple as that. But poor Philip couldn't believe that, so he asked to see the Father! (See John 14:8.) How Jesus must have sighed as he explained to Philip, "Anyone who has seen me has seen the Father" (John 14:9).

In fact, Jesus had said this before: "When a man believes in me, he does not believe in me only, but in the one who sent me.

When he looks at me, he sees the one who sent me" (John 12:44, 45).

What an amazing truth! Jesus was the most complete revelation, the clearest demonstration of God.

But there's more! When did Jesus most clearly demonstrate what God wanted to communicate?

When He suffered and died. One of the most powerful things Jesus' death says is, "I love you so much that I'm willing to suffer for you. I want you back." In the outstretched arms of the cross we see the Father stretching out His arms, pleading for His rebellious children to come to Him.

That event was not for us alone—it convinced the whole universe that God was truly right. He was just. He was love. In His death on the cross, God showed His character in such a way that no one could argue anymore. He vindicated Himself and won the argument that had continued since the devil first accused God of being unfair. The great controversy, which had been fought on the question of God's character, was finally settled.

A minister who conducted meetings in various churches, said that after one particular series, a woman came up to him and gave him a photograph.

"This is my son," she told the minister. "He ran off from home when he was nineteen. I don't know where he's gone. Wherever you speak, would you look for him in your congregation? It may be that he'll be there. And if you should find him, tell him his mother is waiting at home for him—waiting for him to come back. Tell him I'll welcome him home with open arms. I just want him home with me again." And she left, silently weeping.

Just like that distraught mother, *God wants us back just as we are.* He's ready to welcome us and to transform us into His trusting and trustworthy children.

The center of our message

So what are we to do, then? Knowing all this about the God we love and admire, what should be the heart of our speaking for God? What is the center of our message to the world? What's most important?

I once drove a lady to the train station—which was only about two minutes away. As she got in the car, she said, "Tell me about this God of yours."

What would you have said?

Some think in such circumstances we should focus on God's law.

Some say, "Preach the second coming."

Some argue for Bible studies on the Holy Spirit.

These suggestions are all well and good—rightly understood. But they're not the *heart* of the message.

No, the heart of the message is the gospel. The good news. And it's good news about *God*.

So, we're not trying to convince people to say yes to a system of creeds. We're not trying to get them to join our organization simply because of our friendliness. We're not trying to get them to become Christians as a way of avoiding the terrifying judgment.

These methods and motivations are not God's way. His way is to show what He's really like. That must be our way too.

The final message, the only message of the gospel, is one that conveys the true character of God in words and actions. We are to make God known just as Jesus made Him known. We avoid speaking evil of God in any way. We will think of how to communicate doctrines in such a way that they will lead people to Jesus. We will try to live so that people can see God in us.

We don't use deception. We don't distort the word of God. We use all of it, not just the bits that suit us! We set forth the truth plainly.

Most of all, *we don't preach ourselves.* Instead, we preach Jesus Christ as Lord. We're just His friends, His agents, His representatives. God, the Creator, has given us the light of His marvelous truth, so that we know Him as demonstrated in the face of Jesus: "God . . . made his light shine in our hearts to give us the light of the knowledge of the glory of God in the face of Christ" (2 Corinthians 4:6).

CHAPTER 6

Hope in the Living God

1 Timothy 4

Everyone in town knew him. He was always referred to as "Old Jack," though I don't know whether that really was his name. Every weekend, come rain or shine, you'd find him at his usual spot near the shopping precinct. And he always brought his signs, which bore hand-painted warnings in rather shaky writing:

PREPARE FOR THE JUDGMENT

BEWARE: YOUR SINS WILL FIND YOU OUT

TREMBLE AT THE APPROACH OF YOUR ETERNAL DESTINY

I don't remember ever seeing the traditional THE END IS NIGH, but I wouldn't have been surprised—his message was the same.

Old Jack would take one of his signs, lift it high, and parade down the street, calling people to repentance. Then he would mount his pulpit—an old milk crate—and harangue the passersby with his visions of impending doom.

Now, I have no objection to anyone making people aware of their need to come to God before the "day of the Lord." But Old Jack's technique just made people laugh. He was such a comic character that *anything* he said was greeted with derision. It was sad, because sometimes he did make sense—most particularly when he was reading Scripture.

One day I stood nearby to watch the reactions. Most would walk on by, pretending Jack wasn't even there. Some would

49

nudge each other and smile knowingly, as if to say, "Another poor misguided fool." Others would shake their heads in disbelief. One man muttered loudly, "What a nut!" And a few would answer back: "What's this, Jack? End of the world this week again? I thought it was due last week, and the week before that too. What a load of nonsense!"

Old Jack would reply with some vigor, raining down threats and curses on all unbelievers.

"Now that's not nice," some listeners would jibe at him. "I thought Christianity was all about love and understanding and being kind to one another. What happened to all that?"

These responses only served to make Jack madder and louder and more determined than ever to get his message of imminent judgment across. After a good bit of shouting, his tormentors would move off and the crowd would thin, the bearbaiting over.

One thing was certainly true: I never saw or heard that Old Jack's preaching converted anybody. I'm sure the crankiness of this believer produced only the opposite result, confirming people in their disbelief.

How often do we misrepresent the God we believe in? How often do our words and actions make Him a laughingstock?

It is easy enough to misrepresent Him when we're working from honest motives. In addition, Paul warns Timothy of the perversely misguided, the deliberately ignorant, and the malevolently twisted. What they convey is a false gospel—which, Paul warns, is really no gospel at all (see Galatians 1:7). Instead of holding to the basic principles of Christian belief, the people he describes to Timothy bring in false ideas and twist the truth to suit themselves. "But in later days," he writes, "the Spirit distinctly declares, certain people will rebel against the faith; they will listen to spirits of error and to doctrines that daemons teach through plausible sophists who are seared in conscience" (1 Timothy 4:1, 2, Moffatt).

Magic mushrooms?

The church today faces similar distortions of the gospel. Many voices claim to speak for the historic faith, each one believing that his or her particular variant is what the early church really believed. Add to these the people who would demythologize the faith, updating it with the drug-induced hallucinations of magic mushroom eaters or the guidance of extraterrestrials— who claim, for example, that Jesus Christ was an astronaut. No wonder the God of the Bible hardly gets a hearing!

It's because of these misrepresentations that Paul writes so passionately about sound doctrine and the need for individual, Spirit-guided study. "Feed yourself spiritually on the words of faith and of the true teaching which you have followed," he counsels, and "shut your mind against these profane, drivelling myths" (1 Timothy 4:6, 7, TEV and Moffatt, respectively).

What is at stake here is the essence of the Christian life and how others will judge it. We must determine that our lives will present the truth about our trustworthy God and Saviour—a goal that can never be attained by folk who use methods like those of Old Jack.

Yet, despite their reactions to Old Jack, people today seem fascinated with the catastrophic. Note the popularity of Hollywood's disaster movies, the science-fiction-like predictions of Earth's imminent end from solar explosion, comet collision, asteroid impact, atomic holocaust, or alien invasion.

The appeal is there; the concept of total annihilation has some kind of morbid fascination. Maybe it's Global Thermonuclear War. Maybe Terminal Toxic Waste. Maybe AIDS II, The Sequel. Whatever it is, there are plenty of merchants of doom to tout its cause.

And this strange fascination seems to have captured some Christians too. There are some who focus on the apocalyptic day of judgment, the day when the elements will melt with fervent heat and the heavens depart as a scroll, the day when all who are left on earth will burn like stubble.

Yes, there is an end-time disaster scenario. But is it the essence of the gospel? Absolutely not.

What is our message?

What is our gospel message meant to be? For some it really is all the future disasters—doom and gloom all round. They appear to take perverse delight in the coming destruction, the fires of persecution, the torture and imprisonment. Some even act as if they would enjoy—like some modern Samson—accelerating the end by pulling the pillars that support society down upon themselves.

Not long ago, someone said to me, "I'm sick and tired of all this 'God is love' business. I've had it until it's coming out of my ears. I want the God who is the awesome God of doomsday." And another person told me, "When I was searching for the truth, I visited all the churches I could. All I got was this 'Jesus loves you' stuff. I didn't want that, so I joined this church."

Some people *want* the punitive vindictiveness of a divine Attila the Hun. They're glad *not* to speak about the love of God, preferring the vengeful Dispenser of Retribution!

But is this our special message? Is it true that our commission has nothing to do with love?

Surely the good news—the truth that is summed up in the person and witness of Jesus—is the same yesterday, today, and forever. Distinctive beliefs *are* important, but they are not the core of the gospel. The good news is not vegetarianism or tithing or prophetic understanding. Most of all, *it is not doom and disaster*—that's *bad* news!

Notice the message God gives His preachers to proclaim: "Comfort ye, comfort ye my people, saith your God. Speak ye comfortably to Jerusalem" (Isaiah 40:1, 2, KJV).

Speak how? Comfortably. God doesn't call for harsh words of strife and anger, but words to bring comfort.

For that is what we all need most—to be comforted. In the words of Tennyson:

But what am I?
An infant crying in the night,
An infant crying for the light,
And with no language but a cry.

Like little children crying endlessly in a terrifying night, we want words of kindness and comfort from our heavenly Father. And God gives us His truth, not to cause us fear or anguish, but to comfort us.

In bringing His message to others, we need to comfort them. Deep down, most people are already terrified. Yes, we do need to talk about Christ's coming and what it will mean for the wicked. People need the whole picture when they decide. But their decision must not be based on fear.

So what should we convey to people? The truth about the kind of person God is and the eternal life He offers.

"Don't be afraid!"

God Himself justifies this kind of approach. Scripture shows that on almost every occasion when He came to humanity, He said, in essence, "Don't be afraid!" He spoke those words of peace to Abraham, Isaac, Jacob, Moses, Joshua, David, Solomon, Zerubbabel, Jeremiah, and Daniel.

"This is what the Lord says—he who . . . formed you in the womb, and who will help you; Do not be afraid. . . . This is what the Lord says—Israel's King and Redeemer, the Lord Almighty: I am the first and I am the last; apart from me there is no God. Who then is like me? . . . Do not tremble, do not be afraid" (Isaiah 44:2-8).

The angel who announced His glorious good news to the shepherds at Jesus' first coming carried the same message: "Do not be afraid. I bring you good news of great joy that will be for all the people" (Luke 2:10).

Time and again the Son of man also comforted His disciples. Coming to them on the water, He stilled their fear: " 'Courage!' he said. 'It is I. Don't be afraid!' " (Matthew 14:27, TEV). On the mount of transfiguration, Jesus touched His terrified friends and said, "Get up. . . . Don't be afraid!" (Matthew 17:7, TEV).

He tells us, "Do not let your hearts be troubled" and "Do not be afraid" (John 14:1; Revelation 1:17).

How can we approach this perfect, pure, and all-powerful Being without fear? The answer lies in our relationship with Him: "There is no fear in love; perfect love drives out all fear. So then, love has not been made perfect in anyone who is afraid, because fear has to do with punishment. We love because God first loved us" (1 John 4:18, 19, TEV).

If we fear God, it is because we see Him as a punishing God.

In fearing God, we demonstrate how little we know about Him. God is not like some angry father who beats his children with a big stick. The love with which God loves us should lead us to love Him in return. And as that love develops, it drives away all our fear—especially our fear of Him. Paul told the fearful Romans, "You did not receive a spirit that makes you a slave again to fear, but you received the Spirit of sonship" (Romans 8:15).

God the Father regards us no less lovingly than does Jesus the Son. Both are equally loving, caring, saving. As Jesus said so pointedly, "I am *not* saying that I will ask the Father on your behalf. No, the Father himself loves you because you have loved me and have believed that I came from God" (John 16:26, 27, emphasis supplied).

Speaking as God speaks

As we, perhaps slowly and hesitantly, come to know this loving, comforting God, we come to trust Him. Then, like Isaiah, we can say, "Surely God is my salvation; I will trust and not be afraid. The Lord, the Lord, is my strength and my song; he has become my salvation" (Isaiah 12:2). Trust takes away our fear.

So whom are we to speak of—the God of torture, hellfire, and damnation? Or the God revealed in Jesus?

The message we are to give is clearly spelled out for us: "Now the message that we have heard from his Son and announce is this: God is light, and there is no darkness at all in him." "The message you heard from the very beginning is this: we must love one another" (1 John 1:5; 3:11, TEV).

The God we must preach is the crucified King who gave Himself for us so that we can live forever with Him. And in preaching this God, "we must love one another"! For this is a nightmare world—and we need to comfort each terrified soul with what God has done, how He acts now, and the future that He plans. And more than this, we need to broadcast that all are invited to be part of this plan, to come to the banquet, and to go home with their loving Father.

Not all will come home. Not all want that. And not all would be happy with such a Father. But the commission is to go to "whosoever will."

Paul told Timothy, "Give them these instructions and these teachings" (1 Timothy 4:11, TEV). What instructions? What teachings? Paul makes it clear in the preceding verses: "Feed yourself spiritually on the words of faith and of the true teaching. . . . It promises life both for the present and for the future . . . because we have placed our hope in the living God, who is the Savior of all and especially of those who believe" (1 Timothy 4:6-10, TEV).

We are not to give false comfort, of course. We may, for instance, tell people who are dying that they are fine, that all is well. They know our words are lies—and those words do not help, even though we want them to. We need to face reality, during the hard times as well as during the good times, and not try to give false comfort.

So people must realize the gravity of their situation. But then we must pass along the true comfort that God gives.

Jesus offered that true comfort when He announced His mission in the synagogue at Nazareth: "The Spirit of the Lord is upon me, because he has chosen me to bring good news to the poor. He has sent me to proclaim liberty to the captives and recovery of sight to the blind, to set free the oppressed and announce that the time has come when the Lord will save his people" (Luke 4:18, 19, TEV).

Doesn't that bring you comfort? He didn't speak of bringing gloom and doom, did He? He offered, instead, the glorious promise of God's comfort for all who would receive it.

To the sick woman who touched his coat, Jesus said, "Daughter, be of good comfort; thy faith hath made thee whole" (Matthew 9:22, KJV).

Of His experience with the weeping widow of Nain, the Bible says, "When the Lord saw her, his heart went out to her and he said, 'Don't cry'" (Luke 7:13).

David, too, spoke of that comfort: "Even though I walk through the valley of the shadow of death, I will fear no evil, for you are with me; your rod and your staff, they comfort me" (Psalm 23:4).

Think of how often God spoke these words of comfort and assurance. To His people in Isaiah's time, He said: "As one whom his mother comforteth, so will I comfort you; and ye shall be comforted" (Isaiah 66:13, KJV). When I see how my wife comforts our children when they hurt themselves or when they wake in the night with bad dreams, I know exactly what God is saying to you and me.

Our friend's return

Our special message is about Jesus' return, isn't it? Jesus regarded that message as particularly comforting. To the disciples, who were grieving because He was soon to leave them, and to us as well, He said, "Let not your hearts be troubled" (John 14:1, KJV). So He doesn't want us to suggest that He is a God of future gloom and doom. He wants us to present Him as a God who is returning for His friends, to take them home with Him!

Remember Paul's words to the Thessalonians? Did he say, "Wherefore frighten one another with these words"?

Or "Wherefore terrorize one another with these words"?

Or "Wherefore depress one another with these words"?

No! He said *comfort*. Encourage. Motivate. Enhearten. Strengthen (see 1 Thessalonians 4:18).

The word of God is comfort. Why? Not just because God says so, but because of *what* He says. What do we believe with all our hearts? That Jesus *will* come back. And we who are alive and remain will be caught up together with all the resurrected Christians to meet the Lord in the air (see 1 Thessalonians 4:16, 17). *This is the truth for the end time.* This is the truth that we must spread to all those approaching the conclusion of this world's history. Not gloom and doom, calamity and disaster, but the offer of magnificent rescue and healing by our great and glorious God!

"Encourage one another and help one another, just as you are now doing" (1 Thessalonians 5:11, TEV).

We are to be children of the light, not doomwatchers. We are not of night or darkness, not of gloom and destruction.

What are we called to do? Stay awake. Keep our balance. Be alert. We are not to be carried away by winds of false doctrine. Rather, we must anchor ourselves and our trust in our loving, returning Lord.

What do we put on? The breastplate of faith and love, the hope of salvation as a helmet.

What is God going to do for us? We are not going to receive wrath, but salvation through Jesus. He will enable us to live in His presence for all eternity. Praise God! What a hope!

So then, what should we do? Comfort and encourage each other (see 1 Thessalonians 5:4-11).

Making God's love tangible

We all need God's love. We need to experience it through the actions of human beings. Often I find myself telling people that only God can satisfy their need to love and be loved. But these words have little meaning unless the Christian community demonstrates this love for the hurting and sorrowing.

Such love even works physically. Alpine medics have found that, when they assign a member of the rescue team to comfort and hold an injured skier, broken bones mend faster and the injured recover more quickly than do those without such direct contact! This confirms our role in helping heal the spiritual brokenness around us, the desperate need to be loved of God.

The simple truth of God's message consists in this love. It's not some complicated doctrine, just the deep assurance of knowing God and all He plans to do for us—and the consequent comfort and encouragement we provide each other. No quibbling, no gossiping, no fighting. Rather, building each other up in the Lord.

The hope we have in the living, loving God leads us to struggle and *agonize*—that's the word Paul uses in 1 Timothy 4:10—to communicate His love to those around us. Leave to the devil the fixation on doom and the wage that sin pays. *God's* gift is eternal life through Jesus Christ our Lord. That's *good* news!

And so, Paul says to all of us: "Practice these things and devote yourself to them, in order that your progress may be seen by all. Watch yourself and watch your teaching. Keep on doing these things, because if you do, you will save both yourself and those who hear you" (1 Timothy 4:15, 16, TEV).

CHAPTER 7

Mending Our Broken Relationships

1 Timothy 5:1-16

Somehow there was never any generation gap with Grandma. She hadn't forgotten the bright-faced beauty of childhood—she still understood the way children think, still loved the things children love.

When we visited, she would hand us a brown paper bag. In it were trinkets, plastic figures, some assorted candies, and a few coins—foreign and "real"—that she had saved. Thinking of the contents makes me smile now, but for us children then, how exciting it was to take the bag and rummage through, wondering what was there!

And she would tell us stories—amazing, incredible stories that held us spellbound. She seemed so to believe them that her eyes sparkled and her face shone with joy.

Sometimes she would launch into a "recitation." She was full of epic poetry that she had learned when she was a girl, poetry that could move and shock and inspire us and make us giggle. I remember "Augustus was a chubby lad / Bright, rosy cheeks Augustus had . . ."—told when we weren't eating our lunch—of this chubby boy who wouldn't eat and who eventually became so thin that he slipped through the cracks in the floorboards.

We ate our lunch!

Other times we would go outside and pick daisies for Grandma to turn into daisy chains to garland the old apple tree like some ancient maypole. Or she would read to us from some dusty book of ancient tales that came alive and kept us eagerly listening right to the end.

Bored? Never! And she was always so interested in us.

But eventually the passing time that grew us, killed her. Yet, even while Parkinson's disease made her voice tremulous and her hand unsteady, she thought of us. The birthday card that had taken her ages to write spoke her love.

And then one day the cards didn't come anymore. And I was brokenhearted.

But I still remember.

The model for our relationships

Our relationships as Christians must contain some of the love and respect I felt for Grandma. "Do not rebuke an older man harshly, but exhort him as if he were your father. Treat younger men as brothers, older women as mothers, and younger women as sisters, with absolute purity. Give proper recognition to those widows who are really in need" (1 Timothy 5:1-3).

How much happier the history of the church would have been if it had listened to this advice! For here there is no ageism or sexism, no discrimination based on length of life or gender. No exploitation of old by young or young by old—or of brothers by sisters or the reverse. The model for all our relationships that Paul is promoting here is the Christ-filled family.

And it is family language that God uses to describe the closeness and intimacy of His relationship with us. In this "relational theology," God is speaking to His friends—those He relates to in this trusting way. "I'm not calling you servants," Jesus told the disciples. "Rather, I consider you friends" (see John 15:15). We are God's children and joint-heirs with Christ (see Romans 8:16, 17). God is Abba, "Daddy."

This last expression reveals the closeness that God desires. We cannot remain unmoved and aloof; we cannot relate to God in some formal, rigid way. Nor can we consider salvation as a contractual process or one that is primarily dealing with our legal status. Rather, *it is being made part of God's true family once more.* God brings us back—and then doesn't treat us as pardoned rebels but as trustworthy friends, part of His universe-wide family.

"Man is a knot, a web, a mesh into which relationships are tied. Only those relationships matter" (Saint-Exupery). In the end, only relationships matter—our relationships to each other and, most of all, to God. For belief, faith, and salvation are not objects; they are intrinsically involved in our relationship with God.

The tragedy of our relationships is that, as W. H. Auden said, almost all of them begin and most of them continue "as forms of mutual exploitation, a mental or physical barter, to be terminated when one or both parties run out of goods."

You see it all the time in our relationships, especially in marriage, that most-aspired-to relationship.

Man says to himself, "I don't want to commit myself, so I'll give objects: money, car, perfume, flowers, gifts."

Woman says to herself, "I don't want to commit myself, so I'll give promises: gestures, words, smiles."

And before very long, everything revolves around the "*quid pro quo*"—the "I'll do this if you'll do that" mentality. And so, instead of a relationship based on love and trust, we descend to having prenuptial agreements, marriage contracts, and other legal documents. People try to deal with one another on the contractual rather than the relational level.

Trouble is, no matter what the lawyers say, you can never legislate a love relationship. So when the marriage falls apart, all that's left is the haggling over the pieces: the property, the house, the possessions, the kids. Note "the kids"—we don't even relate to them as people. Rather, they are objects to be fought over. The tragedy of the ever-increasing divorce rate is not just the results, but also the causes: selfishness on the part of all, a lack of self-giving, a desire to win by manipulation and contractual control.

The divine relationship

These observations are just as true of the human-divine relationship. If we answer the question "What must I *do* to be saved?" in contractual terms, then there is no trust relationship.

And I've had people very directly answer this question in

such terms: "I do this and this for God, so He must do that for me."

This orientation often leads to the divine-human divorce: the human partner gives up on God because he or she has not seen a return on the investment! Our relationship with God depends on how we view Him and on what we are looking for.

So what does God really want? To use the deceptively simple words of Micah: "He has showed you, O man, what is good. And what does the Lord require of you? To act justly and to love mercy and to walk humbly with your God" (Micah 6:8).

The truth is that of ourselves we can do none of these things! Fallen humanity does not have a natural predisposition for acting justly. Neither do we naturally love mercy; instead, we act out of self-interest, living out the survival of the fittest. And what about walking humbly with God? Again, humility is not one of our natural attributes. In addition, walking with God suggests we agree with Him and are going in the same direction—which is not the case without His ongoing supernatural intervention.

So, how do we develop this right relationship with God? Three basic steps are vital. First, we must admit that we are in bad shape. That there really *is* something wrong. That we are controlled by sin, enslaved to our evil desires.

Second, we must acknowledge that we cannot save ourselves. We must admit that we cannot heal the damage that sin has done in our lives and that if we are left to ourselves, we will die eternally.

Third, we must go to the only one who can help us—the Divine Physician—and follow His prescription. We have to allow Him in to restore, to heal, to save.

Underlying each of these steps is presumed and implied a deep, loving, and trusting relationship. Without it, God can do little. What God most wants—our loving confidence in Him as our most trustworthy Friend and Saviour—cannot be commanded.

So, what is required of us for us to develop this foundational attitude?

David shares his experience

In Psalm 51, the greathearted David shares his experience with us. The central truth he teaches us is that we are broken. What can one do with broken things? Sometimes we can try to fix them. But usually if something is badly broken, we throw it away. Broken things are just no good. They're of no use.

Broken. How many of us have really understood that this applies to us, that God would be quite justified in saying, "This one's broken. I'll just throw it away."

Look again at David's words in Psalm 51. The great cry of his heart is "be merciful to me, O God, because of your constant love. Because of your great mercy wipe away my sins!" (Psalm 51:1, TEV).

Can you hear the pain and suffering here? David is desperate to come back to a right relationship with God. He feels *terrible*. Why? Because God has condemned him?

No. He condemns himself: "I know my transgressions, and my sin is always before me" (Psalm 51:3).

Deep in his innermost self, David knows what has gone wrong. He has a tremendous sense of sin—that terrible sickness that leads to death. In fact, it would not be overstating the case to say that he feels as if he were dying.

"Cleanse me"; "wash me." He wants the cleansing that will heal. He wants his sinfulness cured so that it no longer separates him from God, his closest friend. Without that relationship, he is absolutely desolate.

And so he cries, "Create a pure heart in me, O God, and put a new and loyal spirit in me" (Psalm 51:10, TEV). He says, "I need to be *re-created*! Nothing else will do." That's why we talk about being born again. Just to be fixed up is not enough—what we need is to be remade. "If anyone is in Christ, he is *a new creation*" (2 Corinthians 5:17, emphasis supplied). Only God can create us anew!

"Do not banish me from your presence. . . . Give me again the joy that comes from your salvation" (Psalm 51:11, 12, TEV). Now he says, "Don't reject me, God." Jesus knew God's rejection when He took our sins on the cross. It forced from Him the cry, "My God, my God, why have You forsaken Me?" We can experience nothing more terrible than having God give up on us and let us go our own way.

Having sought God's renewing grace, David makes promises to Him—not as payment for God's work of restoration, but as the gifts of a grateful heart. Because of God's goodness to him, he vows to teach others, to proclaim righteousness, to praise God (see Psalm 51:13-15). When we truly realize what God has done for us, we will make the same kind of vows.

So, what *does* God really want? David's answer: "You do not delight in sacrifice, or I would bring it; you do not take pleasure in burnt offerings. The sacrifices of God are a broken spirit; a broken and contrite heart, O God, you will not despise" (Psalm 51:16, 17).

God does not delight in formal ceremonies or ritual observance or painful payment. He has no pleasure in making demands like that on us. He does not want a cold, heartless religion.

What God wants is a broken spirit, a broken and contrite heart. There it is, spelled out for us. God wants us to be broken!

Not very pleasant, is it? God doesn't want all the perfection we think we are; He wants us *broken*.

Do any of us want broken, damaged goods? If you went to the market and were offered broken plates and cups and saucers, would *you* buy them? Hardly! But that is just what God wants. Why?

Because if we admit that sin has broken and destroyed us, then God can help us. If, on the other hand, we come to Him in spiritual pride, then He can't do anything for us.

Fix the old?

How does God deal with broken hearts? Does He glue them back together again? Does He fix them up? No. He throws away our old hearts and gives us new ones—hearts of flesh instead of hearts of stone. New spirits of loving trust instead of hateful rebellion. Hearts that are true instead of hearts that are false.

God is not interested in fixing the old. He wants to make us new. Our old selves are worthless and impossible of repair. God wants to *remake* us in His image, not polish up the old image.

But God can really help us only when we are broken. That's why accepting His salvation is so painful.

In dealing with the proud-hearted churchgoers of His time, Jesus told the parable of the tenants of the vineyards. In concluding the parable, He quoted a strange text from Psalm 118: " 'Have you never read in the Scriptures: "The stone the builders rejected has become the capstone; the Lord has done this, and it is marvelous in our eyes"? Therefore I tell you that the kingdom of God will be taken away from you and given to a people who will produce its fruit. *He who falls on this stone will be broken to pieces, but he on whom it falls will be crushed*' " (Matthew 21:42-44, emphasis supplied).

We must be broken on that stone, or we will be crushed by it. What does that mean? It means we must be broken to pieces before God can put us back together.

"The heart is deceitful above all things . . . : who can know it?" asked Jeremiah (17:9, KJV). God looked at the earth's inhabitants and recognized that the thoughts of people's hearts were only evil continually (see Genesis 6:5). *That's us!* Broken! Nothing good at all in us. In no one. Until we realize that, until we are convinced that we are broken inside, we'll go on trying to handle the problem ourselves, trying to make ourselves in God's image. But we can't do it.

Until we realize that, we will go on fooling ourselves that we're all right when we're not.

God reserves His greatest condemnation for those who are spiritually proud. "I hate pride and arrogance, evil behavior and perverse speech," He says (Proverbs 8:13). Why? Because the sin of pride is the sin that God cannot do anything about. He can't do anything about it because the one who is proud doesn't ask for help. That's why Jesus spoke to those proud Pharisees the way He did—they didn't realize they *needed* help. They thought they were perfectly well.

Would you go to a doctor for a prescription if you thought you were well? To get any help, you must first realize that you're sick. And until we see that sickness each of us has so deep inside, until we understand our brokenness and admit it, until we ask for help with our sinful spiritual pride, God can't do anything to heal us. We must be broken. We must see ourselves as broken. We must want to be changed from our brokenness.

Broken Bunnikins

Daughter Rebekah came to me in tears. She had tripped and fallen while carrying her favorite plate.

"I fell over, and Bunnikins is broken. Look, he's all in pieces."

Sure enough, the rabbit picture on the plate had been shattered.

Rebekah held out the bits to me in her chubby hands. "Can you fix him?"

"I don't know, Rebekah, I'll try."

I did try gluing the plate, but it didn't work. The plate was beyond repair. So I went out and bought another—and Rebekah thought it was a miracle!

For us, the truth is that Jesus can really replace our brokenness—and more! "The Lord is close to the brokenhearted and saves those who are crushed in spirit" (Psalm 34:18). Jesus came to "bind up the brokenhearted" (Isaiah 61:1)—to heal the damage of sin.

Broken! That is the message. That is the necessity. That is where we all must be. Only then can God take us and heal us and give us what we need for all eternity: a heart that will be forever true.

Only as we understand our brokenness and stop play-acting will we relate to each other as brothers and sisters in Christ (see again 1 Timothy 5:1, 2). Only then will we have the right kind of relationships in the church and with every other human being. And only then will we rightly come to God for what we most need—the loving acceptance and healing of our gracious heavenly Father, the One who binds up the brokenhearted.

May we be broken on the Rock Christ Jesus. May we never be proud of ourselves. And may we all be remade, made new, by the gracious hand of our loving Creator God.

8/20

CHAPTER 8

The Christian and the Sin Problem

1 Timothy 5:17-25

How excited six-year-old Maria was! Her uncle had found buried treasure; at least, that's what it seemed. This treasure wasn't buried in some field or hidden on some sunken wreck, but enclosed deep in a piece of equipment he'd been dismantling. Maria's uncle was in the scrap-metal business.

The village they lived in was like a million others—somewhere to escape from. Maria's uncle had often dreamed of getting away from the poverty and squalor, dreamed of building a new life in a better place. Now it seemed he had the chance—and not he alone, but all his family too!

The means had come through his most recent purchase: some old hospital equipment. Slowly but surely the heavy equipment had come apart: the casing, the weighty lead shielding—which would fetch a good price—and next, the more intricate mechanisms inside.

Then he saw the treasure. Hidden deep inside the machinery he found a lump of glittering metal that looked like bright silver. He pulled it out for a closer look. This had to be worth something!

He called the family together. Their eyes grew big as he showed them the treasure. They passed it round excitedly, with "oohs" and "aaahs" as the light sparkled on the glittering prize. Finally luck was with them. They were rich!

Maria was particularly attracted to it. Drawing it across her skin, she saw that it left a brilliant, twinkling line, just like carnival paint. And even better than that—it shone in the dark! In an ecstasy of delight the family went to sleep, knowing that their fortune was made. They dreamed of moving, of a better home, of a good education for Maria. At last they had something to smile about.

But the next day some of the family felt sick. Four days later, Maria and three other family members were dead, and another 249 people who had come to see the "treasure" were hospitalized with symptoms varying from stomach complaints to great gaping sores.

The hospital equipment Maria's uncle had purchased was an old piece of radiotherapy apparatus, and the "wonderful, lucky find" was a lump of the lethal radioactive isotope cesium-137. Oh, the tragedy of lives destroyed and blighted by invisible yet deadly radiation—the deceptive attractiveness of the agent of death!

This incident paints a powerful and disturbing picture of what sin is and what it does to us. The difference lies in that all of us have chosen this deadly path of rebellion, of walking away from God, of refusing His offer of a cure from this lethal spiritual poison.

More than a toxic substance

Of course, sin is more than a toxic substance. It has its origins in the breaking of the relationship with God. The first sinner, Lucifer, decided he didn't need God. And then Adam and Eve decided to trust Lucifer rather than God.

God's leadership and government were challenged. He was accused of making arbitrary and impossible laws. He was denounced as hostile, cruel, severe, and as being utterly selfish Himself. And the record of time since then is that of God, the defendant, vindicating Himself of the accusations of the Accuser.

So it's not surprising that those who love God and agree with Him should also be the objects of accusations of sin. Church leaders have always been in the devil's firing line—as I know personally!

In today's society, which appears to nurture a malicious delight in the fall of heroes from grace, Paul's words are truly appropriate: "Do not entertain an accusation against an elder unless it is brought by two or three witnesses" (1 Timothy 5:19). Church leaders deserve the support of the membership.

With that said, the sad truth is that, like all Christians, church leaders are subject to passions and temptations. And Paul gives clear instructions for dealing with those leaders who fall to them: "Those who sin are to be rebuked publicly." "Do not share in the sins of others." "The sins of some men are obvious . . . ; the sins of others trail behind them" (1 Timothy 5:20, 22, 24).

All sin—whether of church leaders or members—is bad. Think of the blackest, darkest night. The night of sin is darker than this. Think of the strongest pain. The pain of sin is greater than this. Think of the saddest time imaginable. The sadness of sin is worse than this.

In fact, if you dwell too long on the depth of sin, you will be overcome by despair and depression. *Sin is worse than you could ever imagine.*

Why? Because it works in direct opposition to our loving, caring God. It is the negative of all that is good. It is perversion so deep and so terrible that it caused the death of Jesus Himself.

Remember this when you rationalize that little sin you want to do isn't so bad. It *is*!

Every time you sin, you:

• fight on the devil's side against God.
• increase the agony of a loving, caring God.
• prove the truth of Satan's lies.
• crucify afresh the Son of God.

That's why John takes such a strong stance against even the "tiniest" sin: "He who does what is sinful is of the devil, because the devil has been sinning from the beginning" (1 John 3:8).

We cannot afford to go soft on sin. It *is* appalling. It *is* ugly. It *is* evil. None of our rationalizations must dim our eyes to its terrible nature. "The alienation of man from God is a fact. It is our business not to deny it but to end it" (William Temple).

The fulmars' defense

In my teens I was very much involved in ornithology. One summer a group of us "birders" traveled to the Shetland Islands north of Scotland. There we banded as many birds as we could.

We hoped to advance scientific knowledge by determining the birds' longevity, the distances they traveled, and so on.

Of course, before we could band the birds, we had to catch them. Using Norse *fleyg* nets—which resemble giant butterfly nets—we pulled the puffins and other auks out of the air as they circled by the cliff edge. The skuas, or jaegers, we banded as chicks in their moorland nests. While we did so, their parents bombed us from above, sometimes drawing blood from our unprotected heads. A hazardous activity, studying birds!

But it was banding the fulmars that I most disliked. Not only did we have to climb down treacherous cliffs, but once we got to the nesting ledge, the fulmar chicks would use their famous defense mechanism on us—they violently ejected the contents of their stomachs all over us. For the most part, the contents comprised partly digested fish oil; it stunk worse than skunk spray!

The first time it happened to me, I ejected the contents of my stomach right back! The smell was so terrible I wondered how anyone could ever put up with it. The next time it happened, I was able to control my reaction. Then I became more adept at dodging the squirts, although my jacket still got pretty well coated with the stuff.

Eventually, the time came for us to go home. My friend and I couldn't understand the strange people in the world we were returning to. When we got into the train compartment, everybody else left! And when I arrived home, my mother was horrified. I had to leave my clothes at the door. Holding her nose, she picked them up and took them out back to burn them.

I had gotten so used to the stink of fulmar oil that I didn't even notice it anymore. Likewise, we humans become habituated to sin. We don't even notice how far gone we are, how far short we come of God's glory.

We must see our sinful stench for what it is. We must understand that we have a fatal disease that has destroyed our relationship with God. We must again become sensitive to sin; we must once more feel the pain it brings.

"I do not understand how a man can be a true believer," John Owen said, "in whom sin is not the greatest burden, sorrow and trouble." And David C. Potter pointed out the means for the change in our understanding: "We cannot think lightly of sin if we think honestly of its results."

Dealing with sin

Once upon a time there was a perfect world where happiness ruled and where nothing evil existed. Then in came a subtle being who misrepresented good as evil and evil as good. He invited the innocent inhabitants of this world to try his ideas. He said he was wiser than God, and he claimed that God was selfishly trying to prevent them from enjoying the good things he had to offer.

"Don't listen to God. Just do as I say," said this serpent. "Try it!"

As soon as they tried his suggestions, they knew they'd been fooled. But it was too late—sin had entered the world, and the corruption evil brings had begun.

Now let's transpose this story of the Fall into the key of Redemption: Once upon a time there was a human being who lived in a world full of sin. This being had inherited tendencies to sin; it fell into the ways of evil. But then it was rescued by another Being, who put it right again. It was restored to a loving, trusting relationship with God. Would it want to go back to its old evil ways?

"No," you answer, taking the story personally. "I don't want to go on sinning. I believe in Jesus, believe that He has freed me from the curse of sin and death. But somehow I'm repeatedly drawn back into wrong ways."

So what can we do?

First, we must be honest. We must not fool ourselves that we're sinless when we're not. Unlike the emperor who bought the new clothes, we must not be so stupid as to think that we are righteous when we are "poor, blind and naked" (Revelation 3:17). The sin of self-deception is the worst sin of all, for it blinds us to our problems.

Second, we must sincerely want to change. It is absolutely no use for a smoker to attend a stop-smoking clinic if he or she has no real desire to stop. Similarly, it is absolutely no use for you to come to church or to pray if you do not really want to be changed. For if Jesus' teachings mean anything, they mean that we *all* need to be changed.

Third, we must admit our weakness and accept God's help. We are powerless to help ourselves; we have sunk so far into the flood of sin that without a rescuer we will all drown. Jesus is the one who can save us, who can change us. We cannot do it by ourselves.

Fourth, we must do all in our power to work with God. We must try to avoid situations that bitter experience has taught us will lead us into temptation. We must avoid friends who encourage us to sin. We must avoid those places that are not good for us. Finally, and most important of all, we must come honestly to God as to a friend. Choosing God's offer of friendship places us in a healing relationship with Him.

Into the tank

Another "fragrant" experience offers some lessons about overcoming sin in our lives. During their school days, my father and his brother, my Uncle Mike, visited a sewage treatment plant. As was often the case with my uncle, he went a bit too far—and as a result, fell into one of the settling tanks.

Now for the first lesson: Uncle Mike was in it right up to his neck. It would have made no sense at all for him to say, "I'm all right—nothing wrong with me. I'm enjoying myself in this pleasant place." It was important that he realize the situation called for change. Unless he wanted to get out, there was little anybody could do.

On with the story. My father, being the closest, went to help. He reached out his hand, and, after a lot of effort and struggling, he landed him on the side—messy, but safe.

Two more lessons: To get out, Uncle Mike had to accept my father's help. He couldn't do it by himself. And Uncle Mike had to do something himself. He had to reach out his hand and take my father's hand.

The parallel with our Christian experience is obvious. But the story doesn't end there. We can extend the illustration a little and see what it says about people once they have been rescued.

My father took Uncle Mike home to my horrified grand-mother. But though Uncle Mike was out of the sewage, he was not completely OK. He no longer faced the possibility of drowning, but he was still pretty smelly. He was still covered with muck.

And isn't it the same for us? At conversion, Jesus rescues us from the eternal consequences of our sins, but we are not instantly made clean and pure beings at that point. We are still very deficient! And while God calls us righteous, and He sees us as potentially trustworthy friends, the muck of sin still sticks to us. Before my uncle was clean, spotless, he had to undergo a cleansing process that took time. So too with us. Cleansing us—the process of sanctification—takes a long, long time. We are saved, but God has then to carefully wash away the dirt that still clings to us.

I'm sure that it took a lot of soap powder to clean up Uncle Mike's clothes. In fact, I believe my grandmother had to throw some of them away! Just so, some of what we are, God can clean up. But some things about us He just has to discard because nothing else can be done.

Getting dirty again

So far, so good. We see a little more of God's actions. But what if my uncle had decided to go back to the sewage plant and deliberately throw himself back into the muck and mire. How ridiculous that would have been!

Yet we do that as Christians. We say, "Thank you, God, for saving us," and then fall back into the mess we were in before. So God has to clean us up again. And even then, we make ourselves dirty all over again.

But God does it. He picks us up. He gets on with cleaning us again. He knows what we're like. And although every dirty mark of sin causes Him pain, He continues to work with us and wash us so that one day we will be pure.

But, you say, what about 1 John 3:6: "No one who continues to sin has either seen him or known him"? Isn't this verse saying that if you sin, you've never really known God at all?

No, it doesn't say that at all. It says that if you *continue* to sin, wilfully and deliberately, *then* you have not seen Him or known Him. It's not talking about momentary lapses or forgetfulness or unintentional sin. Those are part of the dirt that still clings to us, the muck that Jesus is washing off.

But if we know what we're doing and choose to sin anyway, choose to destroy our relationship with God, then we have, in essence, thrown Jesus out of our hearts. God will not force us. The choice is ours. We cannot continue to live just as we did before. The old ways must be changed, and we must want Jesus to change them for us. As another version translates 1 John 3:9, "The man who lives 'in Christ' does not *habitually* sin" (Phillips, emphasis supplied).

The key

The key to solving the sin problem is truly wanting the total, healing relationship Jesus offers. It is wanting to live "in Him" so that in every way our lives are born of God. "No one who is born of God will continue to sin." Why not? It is an impossibility "because God's seed remains in him" (1 John 3:9).

We do not cease to be children of God just because we sin. Our relationship to God is not a yo-yo affair—at one moment a child of God, the next moment thrown out of the family because we've sinned. When we sin, we stand in need of repentance, but we are still God's children. You wouldn't throw your children out of the house when they do something wrong; God won't either. But He does say that if we want to, we can leave the family. We do that by choosing a life of sin rather than choosing to follow God and to allow Him to change us.

C. H. Spurgeon said, "Do believe it, Christian, that your sin is a condemned thing. It may kick and struggle, but it is doomed to die." What a hope, what a promise!

"This then is how we know that we belong to the truth, and how we set our hearts at rest in his presence whenever our hearts condemn us. For God is greater than our hearts, and he knows everything" (1 John 3:19, 20).

Instead of looking for the false glitter that is not gold, like the lethal "treasure" that Maria's uncle found, instead of immersing ourselves in the meaningless and ultimately fatal, let us give ourselves over to God. Let us accept what He offers—healing from the ravages of sin and an eternity during which our relationship with our divine Saviour and Friend forever deepens and develops.

CHAPTER 9

Wake-up Time

1 Timothy 6

Highway Patrolman Chuck Downing was enjoying the breeze as it blew up the canyon. He cruised along the mountain road, taking in the view across the valley and back toward San Bernardino, way below.

The idyllic scene lulled him, tempted him to daydream.

Then the blaring of a truck's klaxon horn brought him suddenly to life. The truck raced past down the grade, the driver struggling frantically to keep control.

Downing stepped on the accelerator and sped off in hot pursuit. Faster and faster raced the truck, its brakes obviously useless.

Then the fearful realization dawned on the pursuing policeman. This runaway truck was a fuel tanker—and it was headed straight into town.

Reaching ninety miles per hour on the mountain road, Downing passed the truck. He gradually slowed down, allowing the truck to ride on his rear bumper. Then, with screaming tires and grinding metal, Downing tried to slow the beast's flight.

He held it, but no more. Then, as they reached the valley and the road flattened out, he dropped into a lower gear and hit the brakes with all his might. Shuddering and groaning in a cloud of rubber smoke, they ground to a halt just before the town's first stoplight.

Did he know urgency? Yes, you could say that!

The situation demanded action. No time to dream. No time to ignore the critical conditions.

But sometimes the need to act escapes us. Sometimes we just close our eyes, not even wanting to see. And the demand for immediate action often comes at the most inconvenient moment. But however inconvenient, we ignore it at our peril!

I saw a cartoon strip a little while ago that spoke to our concern. It pictured two Christians lying down. Number one says to number two, "Say something to inspire me."

So number two goes through a whole list of urgent issues: starving children, homelessness, plagues, the Bomb, AIDS, abortion, pollution, and so on.

Number one remains unmoved. "Um, yes. They are important issues all right. But somehow they don't seem to get me excited."

So number two tries again. "Armageddon. End of the world. Atheistic persecution. Torture. Denial of human rights—"

"Armageddon," says number one reflectively. "Yes, that was a good one. I remember getting quite excited about that once. But somehow it doesn't seem to have the same effect right now. I hope I'm not getting apathetic."

"No," agrees number two. "We shouldn't get apathetic."

"No, that would be so negative. I know! Let's just call it faith!"

"Yes, of course," agrees number two again. "After all, God will work it out in His own time. We just need to have faith!"

How easily we miss the urgency of the times and situation we live in!

"UTTERLY URGENT!!"

The president of some company wanted to get his staff to speed up his mail. First he had a stamp made that said "Priority." This worked well for a while—every time the people in the mailroom saw that red stamp on the letters, they moved them through faster. But then they became used to the stamp; it no longer motivated them.

So he had a new stamp made, bigger than the first. This one read "Express." His employees took note and "expressed" the mail through—for a while. But before very long, they were back to doing things the old way again.

Time for another stamp. This one said, in big red letters, "RUSH." It was followed by "IMMEDIATE DELIVERY!" And then finally by *"UTTERLY URGENT!!"*

And finally, in complete desperation, he used them all!

What price urgency?

Like that president, we seem to be preoccupied with time. Maybe that's part of the reason people set dates for the second coming. It's as if we need a deadline before we'll do anything! But such date setting also encourages postponing decision making until the last minute. That's why Jesus didn't tell us the time of His return (see Mark 13:32).

God is not interested in decisions future. He wants decisions now. Decisions based not on our sense of panic, but on the desire to be His friends now.

And even without a deadline, the need to decide is no less important. Let me remind you of the urgency:

"Now he commands all people everywhere to repent" (Acts 17:30).

"Now is the accepted time; . . . now is the day of salvation" (2 Corinthians 6:2, KJV).

"Today, if you hear his voice, do not harden your hearts" (Hebrews 3:15).

"Choose for yourselves this day whom you will serve. . . . As for me and my household, we will serve the Lord" (Joshua 24:15).

"This day I call heaven and earth as witnesses against you that I have set before you life and death, blessings and curses. Now choose life, so that you and your children may live" (Deuteronomy 30:19).

"How long will you waver between two opinions? If the Lord is God, follow him" (1 Kings 18:21).

You can't go on thinking nothing's wrong. You can't go on living your life as if it will never end. You can't go on avoiding the issue, not making a decision.

You've got to decide *now!*

As I heard one of my young friends say to a playmate: "You have to hurry up and love Jesus."

We all have to "hurry up." Not out of fear for the fate we would otherwise meet, not because we're scared of God, but because we want to develop that right relationship with Jesus *now*. If we love Him, we will know Him as He really is and follow Him.

The urgency of hope

It's the urgency of hope that energizes Paul as he concludes his letter to Timothy. Just as he sees the space left on the scroll running out, so he sees time running out. Paul, therefore, crams into this last chapter all the thoughts he can, in a torrent of loving concern, reminding Timothy of the urgency of the time: "But you, the man of God, . . . set your heart not on riches, but on goodness, Christ-likeness, faith, love, patience and humility. Fight the worth-while battle of the faith; keep your grip on that life eternal to which you have been called. . . . Keep your commission clean and above reproach until the final coming of Christ" (1 Timothy 6:11-14, Phillips).

The sense of the imminent coming once again is motivational, the hope of eternal life "at His appearing." This theme underlies all the words of advice, focusing the reader's attention on the joyful prospect of seeing the returning Saviour soon. That great and glorious day is about to burst into this dark world like an atomic explosion.

A symbol of foreboding

Were you ever afraid of the dark? Terrified of the night? Did you call your parents to walk with you up the stairs or stay in your room or put a night light on?

The dark: A symbol of foreboding. The Bible identifies the dark part of the day with evil. Darkness is the time of the wicked—men shall be lovers of darkness rather than lovers of light, for their deeds are evil. Darkness is contrasted with light—and God is light; Jesus is the light of the world.

What's wrong with the dark? What connotations does darkness have?

The dark is a time when we cannot see. We are not made as creatures of the night. We rely on the daylight hours to be able to see so that we can live and work. We are not owls—despite the way some live!

The dark is a time when evil is done because evildoers think they are less likely to be detected when they can't be seen.

The dark is a time when people sleep—for without light, little can be accomplished.

The dark is a time of nightmares and dreams, those nameless fears that are always so much worse at night.

The Bible speaks much about the night and the activities of people at night. Nicodemus came at night to visit Jesus. Why? Because he wanted to keep his meeting secret. Night is a good time for secrecy!

The angel came at night to release Peter from prison. Night is a good time for escape!

And remember the Gospel's fateful words setting the scene when Judas left the Upper Room to betray Jesus? "And it was night" (see John 13:30). Words full of meaning, of doom; words signifying the climax of Jesus' work and Judas's final, terrible choice.

Why speak of all this? Because it's becoming very clear that we are living in the sunset time of this world's history. The light is fading, and the years ahead look dark and foreboding. As the sunset flames, the storm clouds are gathering.

One hardly needs to analyze the news to realize the situation. Even many people who do not accept Bible truth are aware of the tremendous problems facing the world, aware of the way in which things are going.

In a few short years we shall arrive at the portentous year 1999. I have no message about dates, but as the millennium closes, it's interesting to look forward.

At the end of the year 999, the churches were full of terrified people wondering whether doom was about to break upon them. It is said that as the church bells tolled the passing of the year at midnight on December 31, 999, people fell dead of fright!

So what of 1999? What kind of millennium is about to dawn?

Plenty of modern-day "prophets" are more than ready to describe their vision of the future: the mystic dawn of the "Age of Aquarius" or the apocalyptic destruction of the planet, the great advance of the scientific civilization or the descent into barbarism. Then there are those who see the insoluble problems of famine and disease and pollution, and who prophesy that the end will come not with a bang, but with a whimper.

Knowing what the future of the world is and that it is all in God's hand, we may not accept these analyses. But as we look forward, what do we see and what do we hope for? If the situation of this world is getting darker—and I most definitely believe it is—then where do we stand?

Night is coming

"Night is coming, when no one can work" (John 9:4). True? Yes, most certainly. So what are we to do in the meanwhile? Work while we have the light. We still do have the light for the moment, so let us make sure we use it to do all we can.

And seeking for decisions is all the more urgent because of all the distractions—the other kinds of "living" that are so common today. "The love of money is the root of all evil things, and there are some who in reaching for it have wandered from the faith and spiked themselves on many thorny griefs" (1 Timothy 6:10, NEB). Spiked on the same spike where they spiked their bills! In such a lifestyle, there can be no real satisfaction. As Paul goes on, "Instruct those who are rich in this world's goods not to be proud, and not to fix their hopes on so uncertain a thing as money, but upon God" (1 Timothy 6:17, NEB).

The real hope is in God himself—in "the appearing of our Lord Jesus Christ. For at its appointed time, this will be brought about by the blessed and only Sovereign, the King of kings and Lord of lords" (1 Timothy 6:16, Weymouth).

We don't need someone to tell us about times and dates, do we? As good Bible students, we know the Bible prophecies, we know about the future: the coming time of trouble, the arrival of the Antichrist, the religious persecution, and the death decree. Surely, we know all that.

For all of that is involved in the end-time message. How does Jesus come? Like a thief in the night. Secretly then? No. Dishonestly? Definitely not! He comes *unexpectedly!* Jesus comes "in the time when you think not." What will people be saying? "Peace and safety"! (see 1 Thessalonians 5:2, 3).

We need to understand "the present time." Now, more than ever before, "the hour has come for you to wake up from your slumber, because our salvation is nearer now than when we first believed. The night is nearly over; the day is almost here" (Romans 13:11, 12).

So where do we stand? Not in darkness. We should not be surprised. We should *know* the signs of the times, we should *know* the situation, and, most of all, we should *know* our returning Lord and Friend. We are sons of the light and of the day. We do not belong to the night or to the darkness.

We have nothing to do with the night, the reign of the prince of darkness. So we should not be like those whose realm that is. And what are the night people doing? Sleeping, getting drunk. No—we belong to the day. And God holds out the promise to all his faithful day-children that *we shall live with Him forever!* (see 1 Thessalonians 5:4-11).

What a wonderful hope! What a blazing light held out as night descends around us. We have nothing to fear for the future as long as we walk in the light, as long as we follow the lead of the Lord of light.

The fresh fruit shop

In view of the descending darkness, what are we to do? What is our work? How should we deliver the message entrusted to us? Shall we advertise and media-ize and sloganize?

There was once a man who had a fruit shop. He sold beautiful, delicious fruit. One day he wanted to make sure others knew about his wares, so he painted a big sign and put it outside his shop:

BUY YOUR FRESH FRUIT HERE

A man came into the shop. "It's about your sign," he said.

"Yes?" said the shopkeeper. "What about it?"

"Well," said the visitor, "you don't really need to say BUY *YOUR* FRESH FRUIT HERE, do you? Once they've bought it, it will be theirs, won't it?"

So the shopkeeper painted out the word *YOUR*. The sign now read BUY FRESH FRUIT HERE.

The next day the man came back. "It's about the sign."

"Oh," said the shopkeeper. "What's the matter with it?"

"Well," said the man, "you don't really need to say the word

BUY, do you? People know that this is a store."

So the shopkeeper painted out the word *BUY*. The sign now read FRESH FRUIT HERE.

The next day the visitor called again about the sign. "You hardly need to say *HERE*, do you? After all, it wouldn't be referring to anywhere else, would it?"

So the shopkeeper painted out the word *HERE*. The sign now read FRESH FRUIT.

The man came back again. "About the sign," he said. "You don't sell bad, moldy fruit, do you? So you hardly need the word *FRESH*."

So the shopkeeper painted out the word *FRESH*. The sign now read only FRUIT.

The following day the visitor returned once more. "The sign—" he said for the last time. "You sell only fruit here, don't you? And everybody can plainly see that fruit is on sale. So why do you need the word *FRUIT*?"

So the shopkeeper went outside and took the sign down.

And did the people stop coming? No! They still came to buy the fruit, all juicy and fresh, because they knew the man and they knew what he sold.

Now if you can't see the parallel, I'm a bad storyteller. For we have something far more wonderful to give to people than the best fruit in the world. The fruit we have to market is the salvation that God has entrusted to us to share with others. So how shall we market it? Shall we put up signs? Advertise our wares? Or shall we busy ourselves giving people what they really need: God's fruit, which they will accept because they've come to know us, and they realize that they desperately need what we've got!

Now is our time of opportunity, a time for sharing the gospel in a practical way with all those around us who are starving for the truth about God and His salvation.

What is the urgency? The need to be friends with God *now!*

And what we most need to do our job well is not more money to advertise or to put on bigger and better evangelistic programs. Rather, we need to be so close to our loving Lord that we reveal Him to all around us. Our lives should be crying out "FRUIT!"

Finally, Paul wrote to Timothy, put your hope in God (see 1 Timothy 6:17), and grace be with you (see 1 Timothy 6:21)—the hope and the grace of the soon-returning Lord. Slave or free, rich or poor, high or low—God's invitation comes to all. This awesome and incredible Being, "who alone is immortal and who lives in unapproachable light, whom no one has seen or can see" (1 Timothy 6:16), says, "Come to me, my friend."

What's your response?

CHAPTER 10

8/29/93

Choose!

Titus 1

Picture a day in late September—soft, warm, and bright. In the early evening, autumn gold is everywhere, deeper than summer and the better for being unsought.

Searching the brambles round the lake shore, a man, woman, and child hunt blackberries among the thorns. Just now they are a family full of life's goodness, the goodness of God.

Over the shimmering lake, the sun spreads a sparkling net, as if trying to catch the jumping fish. Swallows and martins splash down, flittering on a thousand wings as their summer ends—before the long, long migration begins.

The boy laughs. Everywhere he looks, life is crammed full of wonder. He stops to watch a water rat paddling toward the shore. "Look, Mummy, look," he cries. A pheasant crows out in excitement, rabbits skipscamper about, and the boy points and shouts.

The air is still, expectant, waiting.

It is ready for a better place, an earth made new, when a family is together forever, when God shall be with them and be their God. A time when even this autumn beauty will seem like faded leaves, shriveled and brown. A time when blackberry picking will not be marred by thorns that rip and cut.

The path leads on. The sun falls low among the oaks, blazing the leaves. The swallows stop their playing to gather on the wires, still chittering. Ready to leave. The berry basket is full.

The sun has gone. The path leads home. And the day has ended. The father calls: "Are you ready? It's time to go."

Are you ready?

Are you ready?

A question for all of us. As the Father calls us, saying it's time to go, are we ready to choose to go?

God offers us His eternal life in His glorious presence. Would we prefer to stay here, picking the blackberries among the thorns? Or are we so busy admiring the sunset that we don't realize that the day is almost over, and we will *have* to choose what we will do, how we will answer?

My two children are just like that. Tell them they have to *choose* what they want to do next, and they'll often ignore the statement. They're happy playing, and that's it!

Are we so happy playing here that we're not ready to make our decision? Are we so ready to give up on God's eternal life? What will we choose? Paul emphasizes the need to choose as chosen people:

"I was *chosen* and sent to help the faith of God's *chosen* people and to lead them to the truth taught by our religion, which is based on the hope for eternal life" (Titus 1:1, 2, TEV, emphasis supplied). See what he says! Choices, and the basis for our religion—*eternal life!* How can we be so indolent, lethargic, slothful? How can we be so slow to decide for God's eternal life?

This is "the knowledge of the truth that leads to godliness—a faith and knowledge resting on the hope of eternal life, which God, who does not lie, promised before the beginning of time" (Titus 1:1, 2).

Practical hope

But let's see how this is put into practice. If we have such a hope, based on the promise of God himself (remember John 14, and remember He can't lie!), what kind of persons are we as a result?

Titus was working in Crete. And what national characteristics did Cretans apparently have (see Titus 1:12, 13)? No wonder Paul was concerned to give explicit instructions! And remember, the description Paul gives Titus of an elder applies to all members. It illustrates the results of God working in our lives.

The situation there in Crete was difficult. Some half-converted members were trying to lead the church back to Jewish practices, which had been superseded by the Cross (see Titus 1:14-16). Paul is saying that there is no point in our following the kind of people who claim to know God, but whose actions prove they do not. Instead, we hold on to the true gospel that we first believed—and Paul spells out what this "sound doctrine" is.

Similar in basis and context to the advice he gave to Timothy, Paul is here telling Titus how to choose leaders in the church. The reasons for choice are clear, for once again there has to be a clear distinction between those who follow Jesus and those who do not (Titus 1:5-9).

Instead of repeating an analysis, let's look deeper at the motives and results of such choices—made not only by elders, but by each Christian who chooses God. Paul also speaks out strongly against those who are "counterfeit Christians" (Phillips' term) and the kind of natures unregenerate humanity reveals. (Titus 1:10-16).

So how do we choose which side we're on?

Jesus' invitation

Jesus walked this earth and invited His contemporaries:

Matthew 4:19, 20 (to Simon Peter and Andrew): "Come, follow me, . . . and I will make you fishers of men." Follow Me. Decide for Me. Come with Me and live as I tell you.

Matthew 9:9 (to Matthew): "Follow me." Commit yourself to Me. Make your own personal decision to be with Me.

John 1:43 (to Philip): "Follow me." I'm going; accompany Me. Talk with Me on the way. Take My route.

John 21:19 (to Peter, at the very end): "Follow me." Do as I say. Obey My words. Make your response right now.

Following for benefit

And many people followed Jesus for a time. They saw some immediate benefit from following this preacher. The lame walked. The blind saw. The hungry ate. The dead lived. They followed Him, wondering about this man who could teach and heal as if He were God Himself. Miracles, signs, wonders every day, right there in front of their eyes. No wonder that they followed this miracle man, this born leader, this man who would lead them to victory! They followed Him all right!

Some left home and family. Some left business and livelihood. Some didn't have much to leave at all, but each chose to follow Him, for whatever reason.

Responding to the invitation

And so they walked down the road with Him. And as they walked, they talked. Look at the three responses to Jesus' invitation.

Response 1. "As they went on their way, a man said to Jesus, 'I will follow you wherever you go'" (Luke 9:57, TEV). *The confident assurance of the zealot.* "I'm going through with You. I'm dedicated, Lord. I've staked all on You." Like Peter—"I can handle it, Lord. Whatever's coming up, I'll be there. Don't You worry, Lord, I'll never leave You."

And maybe you already hear the echo of the cock crowing.

An emotional, enthusiastic decision is not enough. The commitment must be made in the cold light of a dull Galilean morning, sleeping out rough on the stony ground, hungry and thirsty and tired, and having nowhere to go.

In his proverblike reply, Jesus reminds the man that this is not the easy choice: "The Son of Man has no place to lie down and rest" (Luke 9:58, TEV). "Don't follow Me unless you're prepared for all this. It's no bed of roses. And if you're following Me for what you hope to get out of it, forget it. There's no earthly reward for you, only hostility, pain, and death. This is the way of the Cross."

And many turned away from Him, because He didn't live up to their expectations. He didn't always feed them miraculously. He wasn't willing to accept their idea of kingship, to take up the physical struggle against the Romans. He didn't say the things they wanted to hear. His popularity waned, and His followers drifted away.

Response 2. "Sir, first let me go back and bury my father" (Luke 9:59, TEV). *Putting it off.* "Lord, I'd like to follow You but . . . I have higher priorities. I'll fit You in, Lord, whenever I can. I can't just up and leave right now. I can't decide to follow You just like that. I have things to do first, to set my affairs in order before I can come with You."

Right enough, we might agree. We don't want to upset the boat. After all, Christianity needs to be fitted in to the rest of life, doesn't it? We don't want to be fanatical, do we?

I know people who have waited until they retired before they were baptized and joined the church. Why? Because of work problems, because they didn't want to commit themselves until they finished working. And that's all right, isn't it? After all, there's time. The Lord will wait for us, won't He?

We act like the man going to bury his father—when the father hasn't even died yet!

In what seems to be a hard response, Jesus tells him, "Let the dead bury their own dead. You go and proclaim the Kingdom of God" (Luke 9:60, TEV). "Forget it. You have to decide right now where your priorities lie. You just haven't got the time to concern yourself about the dead. Your job is preaching the good news of the kingdom. All other things are incidental. Your reply is just an excuse to put off your decision."

Are we home waiting to bury the dead things of our existence? The monotonous routine of daily life, the getting, the spending— they are all just excuses when we use them to avoid deciding to follow Jesus.

Response 3. "I will follow you, sir; but first let me go and say good-bye to my family" (Luke 9:61, TEV). *Family calls.* That seems fair enough, doesn't it? "Just let me go home and say good-bye. It seems hardly right just to scribble a note or send a message with a boy. A few fond farewells, Lord, and I'll be there with You. You believe in the importance of the family, don't You, Lord? We wouldn't want them worrying."

But Jesus looks for the deeper reason. "Anyone who starts to plough and then keeps looking back is of no use for the Kingdom of God" (Luke 9:62, TEV). Looking into the man's heart, He sees more excuses for not deciding. You know what it's like when you go home. Mum or wife says, fix the door hinges or do the laundry first. Oh, and can you first earn some money if you're leaving— otherwise how will we survive? And then the children want some attention. Quickly we become trapped back into the responsibilities of living—important, but not supreme. How many excuse themselves from following Jesus on family grounds?

Someone looking backward while ploughing is fit for nothing. A crooked furrow, maybe even a foot hurt by the plough! To plough straight you have to fix your eyes on the far side of the field and always aim at that point, never getting distracted. Those who look back on the way to the kingdom will be like Lot's wife. All distractions must be ignored, and we must look to Jesus, the author and finisher of our faith.

Making decisions. Choosing. The necessity of making an immediate response. For when Jesus says "Follow Me" we must decide. We've just looked at three ways of making the wrong decision:

— Looking to see what we can get out of it, making a superficial decision.

— Delaying the decision by claiming prior commitments, making excuses.

— Excusing ourselves because of our responsibilities to others.

All this is poison to our decision making! You see, whatever we use to delay or excuse or avoid making a definite and sincere decision to follow Jesus is as deadly as the most potent poison. Spiritual cyanide!

Why?

Because we must decide straight away. We simply don't know what the future holds for us. For how much life does any of us have? We don't have yesterday, we don't have tomorrow, we have only today. And even there, we just don't know how much we have.

This is not being morbid or employing scare tactics. The command of Jesus is: "Follow me"—NOW!

"I am the light of the world. The man who follows me will never walk in the dark but will live his life in the light" (John 8:12, Phillips). The decision to follow Jesus means eternal life. But you only have now to decide to accept that light!

You are going to have the light just a little while longer.

Walk while you have the light, before darkness overtakes you. The man who walks in the dark does not know where he is going. Put your trust in the light while you have it, so that you may become sons of light (John 12:35, 36).

You don't know how much longer you'll have the opportunity to enter into this marvelous light. But if you decide to follow Jesus, right now, you will be with Him now and forever.

"My sheep listen to my voice; I know them, and they follow me. I give them eternal life, and they shall never die" (John 10:27, 28, TEV). We must follow Him.

But far too often, we've misplaced our trust. We've believed the one who can never be trusted. The devil has fooled us all. And through his efforts we have smeared ourselves with dirt and thought we were clean. We have placed our confidence in the Deceiver, who has done so well that not only have we messed ourselves up, but we've often blamed God for it too!

What was it the serpent said? Something like: "Don't worry about eating the fruit. It won't hurt you. And God won't mind. Trust me. After all, it's only a game."

So whom do we believe and follow?

There are many rebellious people, mere talkers and deceivers. . . . They claim to know God, but by their actions they deny him. They are detestable, disobedient and unfit for doing anything good (Titus 1:10-16).

Whom do we willingly follow? Whom do we trust? And how much time do we have to make up our minds?

Decision day

In my early teens I bought a book called *Dawn of D-Day*—the story of the first day of the Allied invasion of Normandy. From a number of eyewitness accounts, the book showed how this decisive battle began. I don't want to glorify war, but this is a good example of determined decision making.

What impressed me most was the Allies' complete commitment. The decision was quickly made, and the whole invasion machinery was set in motion. There was no looking back. The Allies knew they didn't have much time. They made the decision and committed themselves totally to their objective. And many of those who took part made their own personal decisions. This was it. And not knowing how much longer they had on this earth, many took time to put themselves right with friends and with God.

Our D-day is today. This is it! So make the right decision and commit yourself totally to it. For we have "a faith and knowledge resting on the hope of eternal life" (Titus 1:2).

I had a dream. I saw people running, lemminglike toward the edge of a vast cliff, seemingly unaware of their danger. Then suddenly it changed, and I was standing there alone, facing this terrible chasm all by myself. And with a terrified feeling, I was drawn to the edge, and then I was falling forward, out and over the pit of emptiness. I remember screaming and my heart feeling as if it had stopped and my mind fainting away.

And in my last moment, I prayed.

"Lord Jesus, help me. HELP!"

Suddenly I was being carried by two strong arms, being raised skyward, riding high, safe, saved. And as I shouted for joy, I looked into the eyes of my Saviour.

And then I awoke—and thanked the Lord!

Just a dream! But that dream represents reality, my friends. We all face that deep chasm every day. None of us knows how much life we have. How close are you to the edge?

Make the choice now, and respond to Jesus' call: Follow Me! Follow Him who came:

> To show us the true nature of the Father,
> To reveal the truth about God's free offer of healing from sin,
> To transform us into His glorious image.

Choose life, choose salvation, choose Jesus. Choose eternal life together with Him. Trust in "the hope of eternal life, which God, who does not lie, promised before the beginning of time" (Titus 1:2). And face the chasm without fear.

CHAPTER 11

Speaking Evil of God

Titus 2:1-10

In eighteenth-century Formosa, there lived a tribe of head-hunters whose ferocity was legendary. So feared were these people, that to be sent as their administrator governor was considered to be a death sentence. One of their customs was to cut off their enemies' heads to present as an offering to their gods.

Many had come to try to stamp out this abominable practice, but all failed and ended up, more often than not, as victims of the practice they tried to exterminate.

Then came Gaw Hong. Slowly and carefully, he worked to gain the trust of the people. A wise and clever man, he saw that by a process of developing friendship, he could succeed in obtaining their confidence. And the plan progressed well.

Then came the time of the Great Feast. The leaders came to Gaw Hong and told him that they *had* to offer heads to their gods, or the gods would be greatly offended. So he thought for a long, long time.

And eventually he agreed. "But," he said, "you must offer only one head. And it must be the head of the first man you meet in the woods tomorrow."

The leaders accepted Gaw Hong's strange proposal. And the next morning the hunters were ready, hidden in the forest. Very early, a man came walking toward them. In the misty shadows they attacked and killed the man. Then they took the head to the leaders.

And when the head rolled out of the bag, the leaders recognized it was Gaw Hong! Their respected, much-loved administrator. They wept. And from that day on, they vowed never to headhunt again.

Preaching by example

"In all things you yourself must be an example of good behavior" (1 Titus 2:7, TEV). For in the end, all our preaching and professing can be empty words. Like Gaw Hong, we must be prepared to back up our words with our very lives!

Many professed believers seem to think that you can claim to be a follower of Jesus Christ, and yet ignore much of what He said. As a result, the perception of "Christianity" is distorted, making those on the "outside" view with cynicism the pretentious piety and hypocrisy of such so-called Christians.

More than anyone else, God's representatives must understand that God's message is evaluated by their actions. This is why Paul is so strong on teaching the right behavior. There must be a correlation between belief and practice. The aim is to so live, "that your enemies may be put to shame by not having anything bad to say about us" (Titus 2:8, TEV).

For the old and the young, male and female, free or slave, the instruction is the same: speak well for God. Live your lives "so that in every way they will make the teaching about God our Savior attractive" (Titus 2:10).

If we do this, then we are truly following God's desire: to reveal His divinity through our humanity. For the gospel is primarily the good news of God about God. Such good news involves our salvation, but has implications far beyond this.

God misrepresented

The devil's deliberate intention has been to misrepresent God, to make God appear to be hostile and tyrannical—a divine dictator who seeks only to enforce and to impose. In this way, the devil hopes to lead humanity to forget about God, or at least to view Him with fear and dread—or even with hate.

And the devil has succeeded only too well—for so many of this world's inhabitants have only a dim view of God, if they ever stop to think of Him at all. Blinded by the "prince of this world," they cannot see the goodness of God and His actions. They rather picture Him as a being full of revenge, who has no forbearance, no mercy, no patience, and no love.

The sad fact is that the truth about God has been so distorted and misstated that even those who seek for truth find it difficult to pierce the cloud of misinformation that hides Him from their view. Basing belief on speculation and fancy, all kinds of definitions of "God" are given—which is why Paul urges Timothy, "You must teach what agrees with sound doctrine" (Titus 2:1, TEV).

This is no minor matter, for the whole of the Christian's spiritual life is molded by the understanding held as to God's character.

Speaking evil of God

The Christian's aim is to demonstrate in his or her own life, by words and behavior, the truth about God "so that no one will speak evil of the message that comes from God" (Titus 2:5, TEV).

So how do we "speak evil of God"?

"'You have said terrible things about me,' says the Lord" (Malachi 3:13, TEV). Maybe not deliberately. Maybe by simply following tradition. Maybe by just obeying our sinful human nature. Maybe by a deliberate choice, knowing that we place God in a bad light, and don't care about that anyway. What did it say about God when you got mad at your neighbor? What did it say about God when you were found cheating your boss? What did it say about God when you were found cheating on your wife?

In all our sinful betrayal of God we are "crucifying the Son of God afresh and exposing Him to open shame" (Hebrews 6:6, Weymouth).

Even some of God's professed friends let Him down. Think of Moses at the rock, angrily asking, "Listen, you rebels, must *we* bring you water out of this rock?" (Numbers 20:10, emphasis supplied). It was sufficient misrepresentation of God for God to bar Moses from entering the Promised Land.

And what of Job's friends—"miserable comforters," as Job

termed them? Job had been handling his troubles and suffering reasonably well until these theologians arrived to tell him he was being punished for his sins! Once again, in trying to speak for God, these well-meaning but wrongheaded men gave the wrong advice. God had to speak very strongly to them at the end. To Eliphaz he says, "I am angry with you and your two friends, because you have not spoken of me what is right, as my servant Job has" (Job 42:7).

Or the four hundred "prophets" of Israel who simply told King Ahab what he wanted to hear? "Go, . . . for the Lord will give it [the city of Ramoth Gilead] into the king's hand" (1 Kings 22:6). It took Micaiah to say what God really wanted the king to hear!

And then just think of what kind of picture of God Christians have given to the world by some of their actions in the past.

Heresy means death

You don't need to travel too far back into history to find millions of examples. Surely the height of misrepresentation of God is to torture and kill in His name. Sadly, many priests and clergy of the past did not see this, and, in fact, identified with a God of eternal torture.

Through the Inquisition, (known so perversely as the "Holy Office"), through *autos-da-fé* (ritual burning alive of heretics), through the massacres of Albigenses, Waldenses, Huguenots, and many others, Protestants and Catholics, the doctrine of the punitive vengeance of God was demonstrated.

The argument ran like this: if God would burn apostates forever in the flames of hell, then to burn them alive while on earth was a lesser punishment. And if, in the process, they could make a heretic recant while in the flames, they could win his soul for God! That is why in many of the woodcut illustrations of heretic burnings, a priest is depicted holding out a crucifix to the victim, pleading for a recantation. The slogan was, "Destroy a heretic in the flesh for the benefit of his soul."

And as one observer recorded, the clergy would assure the heretic's relatives that while their loved one screamed in agony in the flames, God was pleased with what was happening. Why? Well, because the punishment was for a just cause and, in any case, but a faint reflection of the eternal torture that was the fate of the damned!

Such actions carried out by religious zealots are as far away from the revelation of God in Christ as is possible to go. As Thomas Clarke noted, "All violence in religion is irreligious." As soon as force and brutality are employed in the service of truth, the truth is gone.

As such demonic misrepresentations began, as the sword of persecution was wielded against other Christians, some spoke up in horror:

> It is a fundamental human right, a privilege of nature, that every man should worship according to his own convictions; it is assuredly no part of religion forcibly to impose religion, to which free will and not force should lead us (Tertullian, third century).

> Religion cannot be imposed by force; if you wish to defend religion by bloodshed and by torture and by guilt, it will no longer be defended, but will be polluted and profaned (Lactantius, fourth century).

But the power of the sword was irresistible, and speaking evil of God was the result. How tragic that so many should have died at the hands of those who were supposedly proclaiming the love of God and His gracious offer of salvation.

Why Jesus came
Christ's work was to rectify a disastrous state of affairs, to reveal God as He truly is, to liberate the truth from the rubbish of error and superstition. He wanted humanity to see the true character of God shown in Himself, to restore the lost image of God.

The problem is with us. As Christians, we are supposed to be representing God in our lives and characters. And while Satan has been the author of the misrepresentation of God, we have often unconsciously helped in his program of defamation. All too often, we have remade God in our corrupted image.

So what is Paul saying our "image" should be? It is much more than an outward appearance—it is an inward change of our nature and character. Nothing else will do! Jesus was never interested in fixing behavior patterns or altering external perceptions. He wanted to change the heart.

Christian responsibility

The result of the "sound doctrine" that Paul is telling Timothy about is a life that demonstrates Christian responsibility.

Responsibility is not a very popular word. It suggests things we don't *like* doing, but *have to do* because we're responsible. In fact, many people will do a great deal to try to avoid what they see as their responsibilities. Think of the excuses:

"That's not my job."

"It has nothing to do with me."

"Am I my brother's keeper?"

We're very keen to make sure of our rights, but slow to speak of our responsibilities and duties. And it can be the same for the Christian. We rightly spend much time thinking on the wonderful free grace that saves us, about our "rights" that we now possess in Jesus. But what of our duties?

Now this may begin to sound like the beginning of a heavy sermon! "He's going to hammer us with the idea that we have to be solemn and serious, weighed down with all these dreadful responsibilities. Then he's going to tell us we're bad because we don't do all we should. To prove we're really good, we'll have to come to every prayer meeting, every literature distribution, every church meeting of any kind."

That is not the word of the Lord.

What *does* God say then? How do we understand what God would appreciate from us? The inspired conclusion of David: "You do not delight in sacrifice, or I would bring it; you do not take pleasure in burnt offerings. The sacrifices of God are a broken spirit; a broken and contrite heart, O God, you will not despise" (Psalm 51:16, 17).

If you think you are sacrificing yourself for God through all the many things you think you *do* for Him, then you are only fooling yourself. That is not what God is looking for. Christian responsibility—as defined by God—is not a tally of meetings attended, Bible studies given, hours of Christian witness. Christian responsibility is not standing up and praying: "God, I thank you I am not like all other men—robbers, evildoers, adulterers—or even like this tax collector. I fast twice a week and give a tenth of all I get" (Luke 18:11, 12).

God says to us of the way we understand our responsibilities: "The multitude of your sacrifices—what are they to me? . . . They have become a burden to me; I am weary of bearing them" (Isaiah 1:11-14).

God says to us that our relationship to Him, and our responsibilities, are not based on a business contract. It is not a matter of "you keep up the good work, and you'll get a raise"—a raise that will eventually take you to heaven! The world is too much with us—we think too much in earthly ways, and think that God demands we do the same for Him. Not so!

In a book of children's prayers I came across this gem: "'Dear Mr. God, What is the use of being good if nobody knows it?' Mark."

Do you think like that? No point in doing good unless it is seen, unless you profit by it. Make a big show of all that you do in church. Complain if you don't feel you have received adequate recognition. And if no immediate benefit is forthcoming, then forget about doing good.

What did Jesus say to the "religious people" of His time? "Be careful not to do your 'acts of righteousness' before men, to be seen by them." Why not? Because they look for and get the admiration of others—as Jesus said, "I tell you the truth, they have received their reward in full" (Matthew 6:1, 2). That's it. In thinking how good they are in demonstrating their Christian responsibility, all they have is the respect of others, not of God. Because God wants the motive of the heart to look to *Him*, not to *other people*.

Sometimes we think it's necessary to show how superior our actions are to other people's.

"*I* go to prayer meeting—*he* doesn't."

"Look how she gossips—I never do anything like that."

"I've been in the church forty years; he's only just arrived."

"I'm faithful in giving offerings, but you never see her put anything in the basket."

In all such comparisons we show how shallow our understanding of true Christian responsibility really is.

But on the other hand, neither is it clever and responsible to show by our works how *little* we do:

"I'm not one of those 'Holy Joes' who spouts off his mouth in prayer meeting."

"I give small offerings so people won't think me flamboyant."

"I don't *need* to go to church every week."

"I don't bother with church business meetings because I'm above such things."

"I've done my bit in the past; now I'll relax so others can have a go."

The parable of the telescope

A certain man visited his friend and found him using a high-power telescope to examine the great wonders of the heavens. His friend invited him to share in investigating the sky. So the man peered through the telescope, scanned the heavens, and saw for the first time the marvels of astronomy.

He returned home in stunned amazement after many hours of stargazing. "What a wonderful experience! What an insight into the universe and ourselves! What an unlocking of secrets!" he told himself. "I must get a telescope for myself."

He searched everywhere until he found one. Then he lovingly refurbished it. He carefully cleaned the lenses and mirrors, oiled the mechanism, and then finally put on the lens caps.

Then he put it beside the window and sat down in his favorite armchair to admire it. He was still amazed at its gleaming, polished brass and shining optics. How beautiful it was!

And there the telescope sat. For all its magnificence, it was just furniture. For the man never took off the lens caps and trained it on the heavens. From time to time he would lovingly stroke it, but never once did he actually *use* it.

How like those Christians whose faith is an object of beauty, but never exercised. Like those who claim to wait for Jesus but never look up from what they're doing. Like those "having a form of godliness, but denying the power thereof" (2 Timothy 3:5, KJV).

The Lord's Prayer

• Our Father which art in heaven, hallowed be Thy name— and may we share You with others.

• Thy kingdom come—and may we help it.

• Thy will be done, on earth as it is in heaven—may we do Your will, naturally.

• Give us today our daily bread—so that we might live, and share this bread.

• Forgive us our trespasses, as we forgive them that trespass against us—may it be true!

• And lead us not into temptation, but deliver us from evil— because we want to be like You.

The prayer Jesus taught us to pray directs us to our responsibilities, not out of obligation or the demands of God, but because we truly *want* to be like this. We *want* to have His new nature, which leads us to do the right things every time. We *want* to have Jesus in us so that we act out of love, not out of duty.

So what are you doing in the work of God? How do you dedicate yourself to the service of God? Are you showing your faith by your works? Or have you neither? Do you see your responsibilities?

Have you given up? Are you saying you've done enough? Do you believe it's time to "sleep on and take your rest?" Are you using "humility" to disguise your inaction? Have you done things for so long that you've forgotten the reason why?

Look at how you are and what you do. Ask yourself the fundamental question—what are my responsibilities to God, and how am I meeting them? Not out of compulsion, of a sense of duty, but out of love for the God who loves you *so much*.

I challenge you, and I challenge myself. If we are sincere in what we say we believe, then we should be very different. Not because we feel we should, but because we *are* different—our natures are changed.

We don't please God by service out of self-importance. We don't serve God by doing things to impress others. We don't serve

God by doing nothing, either!

We give God what He wants by responding to His love, by truly wanting to do His will, as did Jesus. Serving God begins by knowing Him, and by wanting to do all we can, not to impress Him, not to impress the pastor (and it's strange how many people want to do that!), not to impress anyone else. The inherent 'reward' is His love, which will, in the end, be made visible in the coming of Jesus to save those who love Him.

When we are this kind of people, living holy lives, being sincere in our teaching, no one will have anything bad to say about us or our message that comes from God (see Titus 2:3-8, TEV).

CHAPTER 12

God's Rainbow
of Hope

Titus 2:11-15

The boy plays in the flowery meadows, his heart full of laughter and joy. The rays of the sun dance with the swaying grass, and soft breezes blow.

The butterfly, golden-winged with silver body, flicks and spins in the soft air, displaying all her charms. The boy's eyes catch the beauty and are trapped. He follows her across the meadows, over the sparkling stream, past the houses of home, toward the trees of the forest.

Soon they are in the dark, deep forest. No sun shines in that dark-fronded place, no rays warm its depths. But the boy still chases his butterfly vision, and he's getting closer. He can see the delicate veining of those golden wings; the silver shines more brightly in the darkening void.

"Here, my precious, my precious," he calls, tripping and stumbling over snaring tree roots and thorn-traps. His legs are cut and bleeding, his clothes torn. But this is nothing, for he's coming closer. Closer and closer, until the butterfly lands on the darkest tree of all, dank and black-moss covered.

"Oh, how beautiful! Now you are mine, my precious." And the boy's hands reach out together, and close round his vision. He cups his hands gently and lifts them to his face. Peering through a crack in his fingers, he sees nothing. His hands open wider. Still nothing. He lifts his palms. Nothing. It is gone.

He bursts into tears and slides sobbing to the ground, resting against the gnarled and twisted bark of the Black Tree. All around he sees only oppressive darkness. Lost and alone, in the dark. And his cries grow louder, full of fear, until he can cry no more. He falls asleep in his nightmare.

Then comes one like a young-old Man, his hair white as snow. The Searcher finds the child and lifts him up.

"Why did you come here?" He asks the trembling child.

"I followed the dancing butterfly of silver and gold," says he.

"Did you find what you wanted?" asks the Man.

"I thought she would lead me to happiness. I thought she would give me all I ever wanted. She was so beautiful, so lovely. But what I found following her was only darkness and fear," says the child. "And now I am lost, completely lost."

"I know the way," says the Rescuer. "If you wish, I will carry you."

And with heart singing wildly, the boy climbs onto the Man's strong shoulders, and He carries him safely out of the forest of darkness, home to His Father's house.

God's saving grace

"The grace of God that brings salvation has appeared to all men" (Titus 2:11). God has not left us alone in sin's night, but has come to rescue and heal us. Despite all our self-centeredness, despite our repeated rejection of Him, God still comes searching, looking for the lost sheep.

And ultimately, to fulfil His promise, God will come finally and completely. Then He will achieve that "coming to presence" that He most wants, and we will be with Him forever. This "coming" God is at the heart of "the blessed hope—the glorious appearing of our great God and Savior, Jesus Christ" (Titus 2:13).

The promise of the God who comes to us

Ever since the Lord God came to talk with the man and the woman in the garden, God has been coming to us. So much of what we understand about God is expressed in this idea of His coming to meet with us.

God came to Abraham, Isaac, and Jacob and spoke with them.

Moses met with the God who came in the experience of the burning bush, and at Sinai: "The Lord *came down* upon mount Sinai, on the top of the mount; and the Lord called Moses up to the top of the mount; and Moses went up" (Exodus 19:20, KJV, emphasis supplied). The entire record of the experience of Israel was one of an active God who went with them, participating in all their history (see Joshua 24: "I took . . . I gave . . . I sent . . . I brought you out"). God came and was visibly present in the Exodus, a fact that was repeated again and again to encourage Israel in later times.

But their faith was not based on past experience alone. The earth-shaking Lord that came out of Edom was to come again (see Judges 5:4; Habakkuk 3:3), ultimately coming to judgment: "He comes, he comes to judge the earth. He will judge the world in righteousness and the peoples in his truth" (Psalm 96:13). But this coming was not to be viewed with fear: "Be strong, do not fear; your God will come, he will come with vengeance; with divine retribution he will come to save you" (Isaiah 35:4). This theme runs through the whole of the Old Testament, right up to the last verse (Malachi 4:6). The God of Israel comes to reward, to judge, to complete His work. He comes to help, to correct, but, above all, He comes to save.

Jesus: the "coming" One

This same perspective is behind the mission of Jesus. In expressing so many of his deeper teachings, Jesus says that He came:

"The Son of Man came to seek and to save what was lost" (Luke 19:10);

"The Son of man came not to be ministered unto, but to minister, and to give his life a ransom for many" (Matthew 20:28, KJV);

"The Son of man is not come to destroy men's lives, but to save them" (Luke 9:56, KJV).

Jesus came for a purpose: "I came down from heaven, not to do mine own will, but the will of him that sent me" (John 6:38, KJV).

"He came unto his own, and his own received him not" (John 1:11, KJV), a coming not in terms of the terrible judgment of

God, but to save us (see John 12:47).

At the heart of the message of God's love in Jesus is that the Son of God came to us, to show us the way, to die for us so that He might save us. He came from heaven (John 3:13, 6:38; "from above" John 8:23, KJV) to earth and fallen humanity. That is the greatest truth of the gospel. We do not have to approach God—which is impossible, in any case. He comes to us. He comes to us where we are. He comes so that God may be with us and save us. "I came . . . to call . . . sinners to repentance" (Luke 5:32, KJV).

Jesus came to represent God to us, and to reveal His true nature in response to the misrepresentations of Satan. By taking our humanity upon Himself, Jesus was able to answer the accuser's charges and to make plain and unmistakable in His life the character of God. In coming to redeem fallen humanity, Jesus showed the onlooking universe the Father, longing to embrace His repentant, returning prodigal children.

And it is the same when applied to the ultimate, consummative coming that is Christ's second advent. Jesus comes again so that He may be with us. We, of ourselves, cannot go to where He is, so He comes to us. The God that comes, always comes to save those who respond to Him. The other purpose is the vindication of God, the conclusive answers of the great controversy. Our salvation is just a part of the great controversy over the character of God and His government.

The movement of God

I once watched a father picking up his son from school. The entrance was on a very busy street, with cars passing to and fro. The boy was looking round, anxiously waiting, his eyes searching for his father's face. Then he saw his father on the other side of the street waiting to cross. He started to run out, but his father called, "Wait there, Tom. I'm coming for you. Just wait right there." After a minute, his father made it through the traffic, picked up his son, and kissed him. Lifting him onto his shoulders, the father made his way back across the street toward home.

That is the truth of the second coming—Jesus lifting us onto His shoulders and taking us home. That is the love, the care, the help of God.

"Coming" describes movement; it involves action. It means taking yourself out of where you are and going somewhere else. All this is part of the coming of Jesus. In John 14:3, he makes this quite clear: He *goes*, he prepares, he *comes* again. The purpose (and the comings of God are always for a specific purpose) is "that where I am, there you may be also" (NKJV).

The concept of God coming down gives meaning to His transcendence, to His absolute power. If there is no coming, no need to cross space, then God is here in the same place and in the same situation as we are. There is no difference. Yet Christ is "from above," and so, in order that He might be with us, He has to come. He has no choice. The barrier is there. He has to cross the vast distance that separates mankind from God. He comes to restore the togetherness that God and unfallen humanity shared at the beginning, the togetherness in which God's transcendence does not need to be shown in distance, where there is no longer any separation because the barrier of sin has been broken down by Christ. The culmination of the second advent is "being with the Lord."

If a man is in prison and I want to meet with him, I have to come to him. He is completely unable to come to meet me. I show my desire to talk with him by going to the prison and sitting in the visiting room. I cannot show my caring by staying at home. And when the time comes for him to be released, I demonstrate my love by going to the prison gates and meeting him there and taking him home for a meal with me.

That is the involvement that the second advent shows. God is telling us something by coming to us. What sort of invitation do you respond to? A brochure received through the mail or a personal call from a friend? If someone takes the trouble to come and see you, don't you appreciate that more? And what would you think of the one you love, if he or she didn't come to you to take you home? In His second coming, Jesus comes for all these reasons.

Coming to meeting

Coming implies that two people meet. When God comes, He confronts us with His presence. God tells us He's coming so that we can decide. We have to choose. It's easy enough to forget someone when he or she is not there. But when that person is on your doorstep, it's a very different matter. God tells us of this meeting in advance, and that He plans to visit us in a very special way.

That is what the message of the second advent is saying. We encounter God, finally and absolutely. We see that meeting, and we should look forward to it. We plan to be ready for the "visit." We look for the signs of that coming.

Imagine the person you love most in the world is coming to your home. What do you do? Excited, expectant, you look up the road, waiting. You clean, you tidy, you prepare. You still have your job to do. But you look, you anticipate.

And the second advent of Jesus is the same. He has sent you a message that He's coming to be with you. You think of that meeting. You plan what you want to talk about. But most of all, you think of the person, and what He means to you. Home coming. The second coming means the eternal homecoming, the full presence of God. And it's personal; Jesus comes for you, and you alone.

Like the reuniting of parted lovers, like the meeting of Father and lost Son, like the encounter of two true friends, the separation is over, the goal is reached, the journey ended. Jesus comes, and the two are one, together; and absence is lost in eternal presence.

Rainbow of promise

I was maybe six or seven. Dad came home with a big smile on his face and a brown paper bag.

"What've you got, Dad?"

"What's in that bag?"

"Please, let me see."

All us kids wanted to find out what he'd brought home. But he just said: "Wait until after tea," and hid the bag away.

"That was the quickest tea ever," said Mother. "Help me tidy up, and then you'll find out what's in that brown bag."

Soon we were all sitting in the front room. The early evening sun was shining through the windows. Slowly Dad took out something wrapped in tissue paper and handed it to me. I tore off the wrapping, and there it was. A triangle of glass.

"Is that it?" I asked. "Just a bit of glass. That wasn't worth waiting for."

"Not just any old piece of glass," said Dad. "That's a prism. Look what it will do."

He took that ordinary-looking glass triangle and held it up to the sunlight that streamed in. On the walls appeared rainbows that moved and sparkled as he moved his hand. Magic! Tiny little ones, medium-sized ones, and one really big one that shone so brightly on the ceiling.

"Please, Dad, let me try." It worked for me too. I could make those rainbows go wherever I wanted them—on the couch, down to the carpet, bounce off the mirror. They would even light up our faces, making my sister's face green and red and blue and yellow all at once. It was really funny looking!

I told her that, and she wasn't too pleased. So she had a turn, and soon she was laughing at me as those shining colors flashed into my eyes like a kaleidoscope in a lighthouse.

"Where did you get them?" I asked as Dad took more of these brilliant prisms from the bag.

"They're from old optical equipment," he told us, "stuff that they're throwing out at work. Nobody wants it anymore, but I thought I'd save these prisms for you to play with. You like these 'bits of glass' then?"

I nodded quickly. "I never thought that just a lump of glass could do this. Oh, look at that one." I picked up another prism that had been cut like a diamond with many sides. In the sunlight it flashed and glowed, and thousands of glittering rainbows spun around the room. "Wow! Just look at that!" I shouted, and we all watched with wonder.

Those prisms became my favorite toys for months. I set them up on piles of books in the sunbeams and experimented by moving one and then another, making one rainbow bounce through prism upon prism until I had hundreds of colors scattered round the room. If the day dawned cloudy and gray, it was disaster—for then my beloved prisms wouldn't work. They had to have sunlight.

But sometimes as the rain came down I'd find a much bigger,

wider, brighter rainbow there in the sky to make me happy.

Then came school and science lessons that taught me how rainbows were made—by the sun shining through raindrops, which split the white light into its different colors. And how we could do this in the laboratory with glass prisms, which took all those various wavelengths in white light and slowed some down more than others, so that the red separated from the blue-violet, with all the other colors in between.

But though I knew how it happened, that couldn't take away the marvel. The rainbow still was beautiful, and my childhood memories of prism playing still live on. For they remind me of the first rainbow—the first time this world saw the sun shining through rain.

Noah first saw the rainbow as he fearfully stepped out onto the wet and muddy earth after more than a year afloat. After his experience, he might be forgiven for being concerned. Maybe another flood would come and sweep them all away. Maybe the God who sent the flood wasn't who he thought He was. What kind of God drowned people as He pleased? The flood had been a very frightening time.

So God told Noah that He would not bring another flood on the earth—and He would put the rainbow in the sky to prove it. This was God's promise to humanity that showed what He was really like—for He hadn't wanted to drown anybody at all. The people had just gone so far from God that His only choice was to save those who would listen and start all over again. He had to turn loose all the rest who refused to listen to Him.

The rainbow is God's promise—that He doesn't want to hurt us at all, that He wants only the very best for us. The rainbow is made by light—and light is from God. That's His nature. God is light, and in Him is no darkness at all. Jesus is the true light that shines in the darkness to show us the way; He is the light of the world.

I still think of those wonderful prisms and the happiness they gave me. Those beautiful colors that made me so glad I had to shout: "Look, Mum, come quick! Just look at these fantastic rainbows."

The rainbow reminds us of God's promise to all of us—and how He has kept that promise by coming here as the light to lead us back home to Him. *We* can be those useless-looking "bits of glass"—useless until God's light shines on us and we reflect and refract this brilliance all around. The rainbow of the blessed hope, of God's promised life eternal (see again Titus 2:13).

And when we get there, we'll find rainbows still there—for a glorious rainbow will be circling God's throne. The rainbow of promise around the God of promise!

For now, though the rain may bring sadness, watch for the rainbow of the promised hope.

CHAPTER 13

9/21/99

The Healing Rebirth

Titus 3

It was just a ten-second item on the morning news.

"A nine-year-old girl was killed on the freeway yesterday. The girl, who has not been named, was struck by a car as she played a game of dare with two friends."

That's all. Horrifying human tragedy compressed into a couple of sentences rushed through by the newscaster. "And now the weather . . ."

As the girl runs, foolish and foolhardy, she is like us all. As the cars hurtle by, as the girl laughs with her friends. Living in the fast lane, excited, having *fun*. An acted drama of the way we are.

Then comes the crunch. The squealing of tires as the driver desperately tries to stop, to swerve, to miss the running child. The dull thud of metal against frail flesh. And life is gone.

For a dare.

And we all dare. Running between the onrushing traffic, thinking we can live forever, thinking we can survive on our wits, our own swift feet. Life's just a game.

Total transformation

Total transformation is what we need. Nothing else will do. None of us have anything to boast of. Whatever kind of relationship we now have with God, remember what we were.

We ourselves were once foolish, disobedient, and wrong.

We were slaves to passions and pleasures of all kinds. We spent our lives in malice and envy; others hated us and we hated them (Titus 3:3, TEV).

A good catalog of the way we all were. Human nature unveiled for all to see.

If you're looking for some kind of analogy for the complete change that God is looking for, then I can't think of anything better than Jesus' words "You must be born again." Nothing else is radical enough!

You could perhaps think of the metamorphosis of a caterpillar from creepy-crawly into translucent winged beauty. But we all know that the butterfly is simply the result of a natural growth process. Eventually, and all things being equal, caterpillars turn into butterflies—that's the way it is. So while there is an attractive parable here, it doesn't say enough. And it doesn't tell of the outside intervention that is so essential—the butterfly is already in the caterpillar and needs no help in the transformation process.

You could perhaps use the analogy of a great medical treatment. That certainly involves some outside intervention in achieving the change. And some treatments are nothing short of miraculous. For the blind to see, for the deaf to hear, for the dying to take on a new lease of life—that's a stunning transformation. But again it doesn't say enough. For it's just a fixing of the defective, a repairing of the damage. The body had the capacity to be as it now is—there was just some damage.

No, the change that God seeks to achieve is so completely different, so utterly transforming, that it is a making new, a being born again. There's no other way of saying it.

And just in case we wanted to take the credit for it, God makes it totally clear that it's all due to Him.

When the kindness of God our Savior and his love toward man appeared, he saved us—not by virtue of any moral achievements of ours, but by the cleansing power of a new birth and the moral renewal of the Holy Spirit, which he gave us so generously through Jesus Christ our

Savior (Titus 3:4-6, Phillips).

New birth. Made new. New creation. New creatures. It is not a fixing up of the old. God is the only one who can accomplish this healing rebirth. And it is so revolutionary that the only way to explain it is by speaking of making new, being born anew, again.

And not only us ourselves. For how can God ever prevent the childish games of running between the cars unless He changes this whole world? The objective is a new heaven and a new earth, where righteousness dwells (see 2 Peter 3:13).

That's the kind of complete, total, and utter transformation that Jesus is talking about.

What Jesus didn't say

Jesus did *not* say:

> Verily verily, I say unto thee, Except a man accept the traditional reformationist theory of the propitiatory atonement in which representative satisfaction is provided through blood appeasement for forensic justification so that the penal demands and requirements of divine justice can be absolved and wrath can be fully assuaged, he cannot see the kingdom of God.

If that was what Jesus meant, why didn't he say it? Or, did Jesus reply to Nicodemus by saying this?

> Except a man believe in the redemptive bargain through which the substitutionary and vicarious sacrifice provided on the cross we are ransomed from the possession of the devil by this legal transaction, he cannot see the kingdom of God.

If that was what Jesus meant, why didn't He say it? Maybe Jesus should have said to Nicodemus:

> Except a man accomplishes his own character perfection and works hard to ensure he is acceptable and makes him-

self a complete overcomer, he cannot see the kingdom of God.

The truth is that Jesus said none of these things when trying to explain to Nicodemus the Searcher the real truths of salvation.

To remind ourselves, what Jesus actually said was: "Verily, verily, I say unto thee, Except a man be born again, he cannot see the kingdom of God" (John 3:3, KJV).

In these very simple but profound words, Jesus explained the key to God's salvation in a way that is far truer to our experience than heavily weighted Latin-derived words (such as "expiatory justification") or descriptions of self-righteousness!

Our "theories of the atonement"—penal substitution, satisfaction, moral influence, whatever—are simply that: theories. God does not provide a systematic theory of how He saves us— He just says He can and does! So when Jesus wants to speak deeply and urgently to those who are seeking after the truth of God's salvation, Jesus doesn't give them a mass of indigestible and convoluted theory, but the basic fact of how God saves us: by totally changing us.

We must be "born again."

Tragically, that phrase has been taken over by various groups and means much less today than it did originally. Nicodemus expresses what should be our reaction: "How can a man be born when he is old?" (verse 4). The idea is totally ridiculous! But in being born again we have the best picture of how God saves us.

He doesn't take us as we are and fix us up a little.

He doesn't just "wash off" the accumulated dirt of sin.

He doesn't provide us with a recipe to follow.

He totally transforms us, so that we are completely different people.

That is the key to Jesus' assertion to Nicodemus. He does not simply take a "reasonably good" kind of object and polish it up a little. Sometimes our images of the washing of baptism suggest to our minds that we are simply somewhat dirtied up on the outside. The truth of the matter is that we are rotten to the core.

This fact Scripture reminds us of again and again: no one is righteous, no not one; all have sinned and come short; our hearts are deceitful above all things, and desperately wicked; all our righteousnesses are as filthy rags—on and on in a litany of condemnation (see Romans 3:10, 23; Jeremiah 17:9; Isaiah 64:6).

Such statements are not supposed to lead to despair, but to remind ourselves of exactly where we are. There is no chance if we rely on ourselves. There is no hope if we think all we need is to be "cleaned up" a bit. There is absolutely no possibility as long as we think we're in control.

"If anyone is in Christ, he is a new creation; the old has gone, the new has come!" (2 Corinthians 5:17). Absolutely nothing else will do! Total transformation, a complete reworking of the material, starting entirely afresh. Only then is there hope, for as new beings we come to God, leaving the dead slough of ourselves behind.

The trouble with our attempts to "explain" how salvation works is that we always want to devise some "system" by which we imagine God works. The difficulty is, of course, that in doing so, we force ourselves to go far beyond what God has told us on the subject!

But instead of viewing the regulations, look at the relationship. What went wrong in the first place? A smashed, destroyed relationship that had been based on mutual trust. What needs to be done? The establishment of a new trusting relationship, just like that new relationship between parent and newborn child.

God does not promise to get into involved maneuvers to achieve legal appeasement or to bargain for our souls. He does promise to so heal and remake us that we can come into His presence as His newborn children, made once again in His divine image.

We must be born again.

The Lord who heals

So what of this God who says, "You must be born again"? At heart here is the direct intervention of the God who announces: "I am the Lord who heals you" (Exodus 15:26).

The context is the healing of the bitter waters at Marah, and is God's self-description. And throughout His dealings with His people, God reveals the truth of His statement time and time again. Far more than an assertion of His physical healing, this identification of God by Himself shows His primary goal of spiritual healing.

And if Jesus is the self-revelation of God, what does His life tell us? What did He spend most of His ministry doing? Not preaching. Not even teaching. Not even performing amazing signs like the feeding of the five thousand. He spent most of His time with those truly meaningful miracles of healing.

And if that is what Jesus spent much of His active ministry doing, what does that say to us?

What did Jesus say He came for? To show us the Father. And by performing so many miracles of healing, what does that say about our loving heavenly Father? That He wants to heal. He wants to cure us. He wants to restore us to perfect health.

Healing the paralytic

The dramatic cure of the paralytic shows us this truth and also illustrates defective human thinking on this topic. You remember what happened. The paralytic was lowered through the roof by his friends, and Jesus' reaction was this: "When Jesus saw their faith, he said, 'Friend, your sins are forgiven'" (Luke 5:20).

We normally interpret this event as proving that Jesus was indeed God—that He could truly forgive sins. And that the Pharisees thought Jesus blasphemous for saying He could forgive sins. But there's more!

Jesus wants to get at the heart of the Pharisees' mistaken thinking. See what he tells them:

> Jesus knew what they were thinking and asked, "Why are you thinking these things in your hearts? Which is easier: to say, 'Your sins are forgiven,' or to say, 'Get up and walk'? But that you may know that the Son of Man has authority on earth to forgive sins. . . . He said to the paralyzed man, "I tell you, get up, take your mat and go home" (Luke 5:22-24).

What is Jesus really doing here? Is He healing the man of his physical disability? Yes, certainly. Is He healing the man of his spiritual malady? Yes, as well. And what is more important? Physical cure or spiritual healing? Are you sure?

OK, now let me ask you: What does salvation mean?

Oh, that's easy—it means we're saved from something. Like people from a sinking ship? Yes, true.

But there's more to God's salvation than that. We have an old English word that is similar to salvation—*salve*. As Jesus tells in Revelation (3:18), we're meant to put on eye salve. Why? To cure our spiritual blindness so that we may see. To heal our eyes.

So what is salvation? It's healing.

Not just being counted legally right before God. Christ's salvation is the healing process, beginning with our conversion and lasting until we meet the Lord face to face.

Two sayings

As an illustration of this vital fact, take a look at two sayings of Jesus. To Mary, who anointed His feet, Jesus said, "Your faith has saved you" (Luke 7:50). Then to the woman He healed from an issue of blood, He said, "Your faith has healed you" (Luke 8:48).

Interesting. It's even more interesting when I tell you that the words in the original are identical—what Jesus told Mary was the same as what He said to the woman He healed!

The word translated *healed* in one case and *saved* in the other is identical!

Salvation means healing. Not so much about wiping recorded sins off the slate so that you can start with a clean slate, but healing the disease—the disease of sin.

This is so important to realize. God is not checking off sins, forgiven or not. He's trying to be like a kind and loving doctor, trying to heal us from a deadly, fatal disease. He is not primarily concerned with outward conformity. He wants a cured heart.

Healing the brokenhearted

Over and over again, Jesus reemphasizes this point. How did Jesus announce His ministry? With the words of Luke 4:18, which was a quote from Isaiah showing the continuity of the healing nature of God: "The Spirit of the Lord God is upon me; . . . he hath sent me to bind up [heal] the brokenhearted" (Isaiah 61:1, KJV).

What a promise! What a clear demonstration of what He wanted to do for the downtrodden, sick, and spiritually diseased people around Him. And what a promise for us too! Jesus doesn't want to just clear your bank account of the sin overdraft. He wants to free you from sin sickness. That is true salvation—for in the end, you will be healed completely, and sin's disease will be gone. You won't even want to sin anymore.

He promises in Jeremiah 3:22, "I will heal your backslidings" (KJV; see also Hosea 14:4).

He says in Psalm 147:3 that "he heals the brokenhearted."

David cried out to God in Psalm 41:4: "Lord be merciful unto me: heal my soul, for I have sinned against thee" (KJV).

And in the prophecies of a healing Messiah to come, we hear: "He was wounded for our transgressions, he was bruised for our iniquities: the chastisement of our peace was upon him; and with his stripes we are healed" (Isaiah 53:5, KJV). "For the Sun of righteousness shall arise with healing in his wings" (Malachi 4:2, KJV).

No question about it. Sin is a terrible sickness of the soul, and God is the only one who can heal us.

Ignoring the doctor

Imagine you're sick. Maybe you don't even know. But the doctor diagnoses some major problem. Do you ignore it and hope it goes away? Do you pretend nothing's wrong? Or do you go to the only one who can treat you and make you well again? Obvious, isn't it?

Whose fault is it if we refuse to admit anything is wrong? Or if we tear up the prescription? Or if we secretly flush the pills away? Or if we refuse permission for a lifesaving operation?

We often hear today, "Oh, if only we could have a true miracle right now. How much easier it would be to believe." But in truth, Jesus' miracles were for one purpose: to show us a loving God. Don't be fooled by the "faith-healers" of the present. In very direct contrast, every miracle that Jesus performed was intended to bring the people to the tree of life, whose leaves are for the healing of nations (see Revelation 22:2).

Christ's presence was healing virtue for the sinner, the transforming power of God for salvation. The same power that formed the universe, that created the worlds and hung them in space, that formed Adam from the dust of the ground and breathed the power of life into that inert body—that same power is the power that transforms us from sinful beings into God's new creation.

Only antidote

God's good news is the only antidote to this sin-sick and dying world. Like a patient falling into a fatal coma, this world needs to know of God's healing power before it is too late. The sin that has severed us from the life of God can only be healed by the direct intervention of the Divine Doctor himself.

For how much more evidence do we need as to our situation? How much more proof do we have to have of our fatal condition? How much more convincing do we require before we will take the only antidote?

Can God really love *me*?

The need to be loved is surely a universal wish. Children may rightly expect the love of other members of their family, but soon find that no one can necessarily expect love from others. Perhaps this is part of the answer to the painful questions of growing up—that we look for love, but do not often find it.

And it's so hard when doubt enters. "I'm not sure whether he loves me." "She says she loves me. I wonder if it's true." One of the saddest bits of graffiti I've seen said something like this:

Kevin hates Jane because
1. Four people told me she loved me.
2. When I asked her, she said it wasn't true.

We want to be loved, but we're so frightened of being hurt. And so we shut ourselves away. We even doubt whether God truly loves us.

"If God loved me, He wouldn't let this happen to me."

"If God really loves me, why didn't He keep my wife from dying?"

So when we read those words "For God so loved the world . . . ," we think they don't apply to us. If you're like that and still doubt whether God loves you, look at the Cross and let me ask you: How much more love do you need to believe God is really sincere?

God poured out the Holy Spirit abundantly on us through Jesus Christ our Savior, so that by his grace we might be put right with God and come into possession of the eternal life we hope for (Titus 3:6, 7, TEV).

How much more could God love you? How much more do you need?

Skepticism and doubt

Thomas was a total skeptic: "Unless I see the nail marks in his hands and put my finger where the nails were, and put my hand into his side, I will not believe it!" (John 20:25).

He just wasn't convinced that Jesus had risen from the dead. He'd listened with the others as they'd heard Jesus talk about rising the third day. He'd seen proof of Jesus' power in all the miracles and divine teachings. He'd believed that Jesus was the Messiah. But this—"This I can't believe," he said.

You may have sat in church for many long years. You may have heard the same things said over and over again. And you may have wondered in your heart, "Is it really true? Can I believe all that?"

Perhaps it's all become a bit too much for you. And, like Thomas, you say, "Unless I have firm, conclusive, and dramatic proof, I will not believe. Unless I see Jesus like Paul did, I won't become a Christian. Unless God shows me a special sign, I'm going to give up on Him." Doubts, worries, questions all prevent us from committing ourselves fully for God.

On the road to Emmaus, Jesus had to explain His mission all over again. They had not believed. They doubted whether Jesus was really the Christ. And Jesus had to speak very straight: "How foolish you are, and how slow of heart to believe all that the prophets have spoken!" (Luke 24:25).

What about you? Is Jesus saying that to you too? "How foolish you are, and how slow of heart to believe!"

In the Sermon on the Plain, Jesus told His hearers not to be of a "doubtful mind" (see Luke 12:29). I say the same to you. Don't doubt anymore. Don't put it off anymore. Decide right now, and say "Yes" to Jesus.

And if there's a little voice speaking to you right now, saying you can't decide for Jesus because you're too bad, just let me remind you that Jesus came to call the sinners, not the righteous, to repentance. Don't let the devil tell you that you have to be perfect before God will accept you. He takes you right where you are and leads you on to righteousness through His healing power.

Don't say to yourself, "I can't become a Christian until I stop sinning."

Don't say to yourself, "I can't be accepted by God until I'm good."

Don't say to yourself, "I can't be saved until I feel right."

Throw away all your doubts. Trust in the word of the Lord, who will save to the uttermost those who come to Him in faith. Believe Him who promised, and trust the God who heals you. Now!

For only a total transformation is enough. We must be born again!

CONCLUSION

Hope:
The Final Word

"More than any other time in history, mankind faces a crossroads. One path leads to despair and utter hopelessness. The other, to total extinction. Let us pray we have the wisdom to choose correctly" (Woody Allen).

As the proverb goes, many a true word spoken in jest. And in Woody Allen's cynical self-mocking of humanity is expressed the "no-way-out" syndrome so common in today's mentality. The scoffers are out in force—there is no hope, they will say.

"No hope in God—for God is dead."

"No hope in humanity—for we cannot change ourselves."

"No hope in this planet we call home—for we are fated to destroy it."

Or, if you are lucky enough to find an optimist somewhere, his or her hope is likely to be based in some New Age mystic paradise or scientocratic utopia or vague idea of the brotherhood of man. All too many, however, have little hope at all. They are saying, "Live for today, for tomorrow the world dies."

Most of all, people seem to have no personal hope. And if there is no God and no future life and no reason for living and no point for whatever you want to do—then maybe there isn't much basis for hope.

Do we have something to say to this end-time world? Absolutely! And what we have to say points forward to a future that denies the bleak nihilism of the philosophers and the carping self-mocking of Woody Allen.

You, me, and the future

What does the future hold for you? That's something we all think on. What does tomorrow hold for me? What is going to happen? How will my life be?

And for us as Christians, the vital question is how our relationship to God will be. We don't, of course, believe once saved, always saved. Nor do we believe once lost, always lost! But surely we need to know the assurance of our salvation now and in the time to come. And that means we have to know about the future and how we will act—and most important, what God will do. That's been the message of this book—as revealed in those inspired letters of Paul to Timothy and Titus.

So let's tie it down for modern humanity in all its hopelessness. Listen to the voices of this world:

Man knows at last that he is alone in the universe's unfeeling immensity. His destiny is nowhere spelled out (Jacques Monod, biologist).

Man has reached a turning point in history (G. R. Taylor, historian).

It is my belief that we have entered upon the age of abandonment, that God has turned away from us and is leaving us to our fate (Jacques Ellul, philosopher).

I have seen the future and it doesn't work (Robert Fulford, writer).

The world has a cancer and the cancer is man (Club of Rome report).

If you want a picture of the future, imagine a boot stomping on the human face—forever (George Orwell, novelist).

We can no longer look for the return of the Son of Man on the clouds of heaven or hope that the faithful will meet him in the air (Rudolf Bultmann, theologian).

It's crisis time, then, for our world. The outlook is gloomy! We are all part of this world, and when we think of its future, we wonder. For the problems it faces and the troubles that we see are so great that only trust in God can keep us from despair.

Read these words by W. B. Yeats from his poem entitled, "The Second Coming":

Turning and turning in the widening gyre
The falcon cannot hear the falconer;
Things fall apart; the centre cannot hold;
Mere anarchy is loosed upon the world,
The blood-dimmed tide is loosed, and everywhere
The ceremony of innocence is drowned.

His image is of coming doom, the second coming likened to some nightmare monster about to be born into this world—a terrifying future of all things falling apart, the world order breaking down, and anarchy running rife.

And so many people are thinking that way today. The consensus is that the world will become more and more crowded, with fewer and fewer resources able to sustain the increasing population, that pollution will increase and the whole ecology will begin to break down. For the millions upon millions of the impoverished, there will be a nightmare of disease and starvation, of malnutrition and death.

Time is running out. That is the message—and as we look around us, we know that to be true. And while we experience the trauma of watching the famine victims die, as wars and violence increase, as pollution and the nuclear threat hang over our heads—we know the real problem is our own: sinful humanity and this evil world.

For if we are not one of God's people, what else is of any use? Paul says that even if he gave his body to be burned and did not have love, his martyrdom would be meaningless (see 1 Corinthians 13:3). What does it profit any of us to save many and make a shipwreck of our own faith?

Later

Like wearing a watch that runs slow, it's later than you think! That is today's message: It's later than you think. Not to make us panic or to create a fear of being caught unawares, but to remind us.

Where are we going? Whom do we belong to? Can we say we are truly one of God's children? Do we know the abiding peace of God in our lives? Do we trust Him to save us? What do we expect from Him?

All these questions that we must answer!

"At that time men will see the Son of Man coming in clouds with great power and glory" (Mark 13:26). What time? Soon and very soon. Jesus is talking about the near future. How do we know? Because this world's troubles are outrunning man's ability to control them. Because the great conflict between good and evil is reaching its peak. Because God in mercy delays no longer than He absolutely has to. And so He's coming—in power and great glory.

God sends out His angels. Whom does He gather? His elect. Who are they? Those who are His friends, those who have taken the time to get to know this loving God who comes for them (see Mark 13:27).

This is our future! Not nuclear war or famine destruction, with the human race dying out like the dinosaurs! Not the horrifying picture of anarchy and disorder, of pollution and crime and violence. There is going to be an end to this world. But the way it will end will be so amazing that hardly anybody can believe it!

But believe it!

So I ask again, What does your future hold?

God's promised future

The Bible tell us very clearly what is going to happen. Our Lord and Saviour Jesus will descend the corridors of the sky to come and take those who love Him back home.

The vital question is: Where will we be? Will we be looking up, saying, "Lo, this is our God; we have waited for him, and he will save us" (Isaiah 25:9, KJV)? Or will we be with those who are calling for the rocks and mountains to fall on us? (see Luke 23:30; Revelation 6:16).

Are we going to have a part in that great gathering call?

Some people collect stamps—the ones they like. Other people collect rocks—those they find interesting and beautiful. God comes to collect people—those He loves and who have loved Him, those God finds truly interesting and spiritually beautiful.

How does He decide? On the basis of our response to His call, to His offer of saving, healing, transforming love.

And so Jesus gives the lesson of the fig tree, with its blossoming leaves. "Learn the lesson," He says. "See that I am really coming soon." And what should you do? Be on your guard. Be alert. Watch! (see Mark 13:28-31).

The only people who will be watching for Jesus to come are those who are really *dying* for him to come! Those who truly love Jesus, who know in their hearts that He's coming to take them home. Do you know this? Are you confident? Are you assured?

Watch!

"Be ready," says Jesus. "Don't go sleepy on God—forgetting your friendship with Him. And what I'm telling you, I tell everyone: *Watch!*" (see Mark 13:32-37).

When you know someone's coming to visit, you don't take a snooze! If the queen or the president were coming to your home, you wouldn't spend your time occupied with trivial things. You'd get ready, wouldn't you?

Jesus is returning, and we want to be ready, for He truly is our best Friend.

Let me remind you of the focus of our attention:

> The Lord himself will come down from heaven, with a loud command, with the voice of the archangel and with the trumpet call of God, and the dead in Christ will rise first. After that, we who are alive and are left will be caught up with them in the clouds to meet the Lord in the air. And so we will be with the Lord forever. Therefore encourage each other with these words (1 Thessalonians 4:16-18).

Some may wonder why God takes so long. And while we try to wait patiently, we can remember, "Hope deferred makes the heart sick, but a longing fulfilled is a tree of life" (Proverbs 13:12).

Others may plead with God to allow them a little more time, feeling that, like Job, "My days are swifter than a weaver's shuttle, and they come to an end without hope" (Job 7:6).

But as the God we know comes to us, as the great day dawns, then we will delight in welcoming our Friend and allowing Him to take us home. This is the everlasting hope.

We do not grieve, we do not live, we do not think like the rest of the world who have no hope (see 1 Thessalonians 4:13).

Hope: real, true, and lasting

Only those who trust God can have real, true, and lasting hope—for only they *know* God as friend, and the future He has planned. God has told us what He plans, and He is faithful to that promise. He has the will, the power, and the love to do it. So despite all the gloomy predictions and the increasing despair, the mindless running after the pleasure of the moment, we can have absolute confidence in the promise of the returning Lord: "We wait for the blessed hope—the glorious appearing of our great God and Savior, Jesus Christ" (Titus 2:13).

Our hope is alive, upward-looking, and absolutely God-sure. And this is the hope we are to remember, to grasp, to celebrate. Before Jesus left this earth, He told us to celebrate His death and resurrection until He comes.

Remember that command. Don't look back; look forward. Forward to that great day of the future when those who choose God shall be reunited with Him to spend all eternity in His presence.

Come, Lord

"Maranatha," said the early Christians. What did it mean? The Lord has come. The Lord will come. Come, Lord.

It speaks of how Jesus came to give Himself for us, how He comes into our lives in the present, and how He will come again on the clouds of heaven.

But it is also a prayer. A prayer that Jesus will come now and forever, that He will take control of our lives. That He will remove our guilt and remake us in His image, healed, restored, and forgiven.

Take the assurance He gives you, my friend. Know the peace of a sure future with God. You have "a faith and knowledge resting on the hope of eternal life" (Titus 1:2).

Don't worry about what happens around you. Trust in the coming Lord who is with us today, and say, "Maranatha: Come, Lord!"

Prisoners of hope

We are "prisoners of hope" (Zechariah 9:12), committed to that glorious promise of God Himself. It is a hope that gives us meaning and purpose, a destiny with our Creator and Redeemer: "We have placed our hope in the living God, who is the Savior of all" (1 Timothy 4:10, TEV).

And "because we have this hope, we are very bold" (2 Corinthians 3:12, TEV).

So "take hold of the eternal life to which you were called" 1 Timothy 6:12).

You need to hope again. You need to recapture the blessed hope, the hope of eternal life, and live it now!